COME HOME, PAPA

Short Stories on Road Safety by Scholarship-Winning Daughters of Truck Drivers

Foreword by NITIN GADKARI

Special Message by ANAND MAHINDRA

AMARYLLIS

AMARYLLIS

An imprint of Manjul Publishing House Pvt. Ltd.
• 7/32, Ansari Road, Daryaganj, New Delhi 110 002
Website: www.manjulindia.com
Registered Office:
• 10, Nishat Colony, Bhopal 462 003 – India

#ComeHomePapa is a collaborative initiative of

#TellMeYourStory A Koral Dasgupta initiative | सड़क परिवहन और राजमार्ग मंत्रालय MINISTRY OF ROAD TRANSPORT & HIGHWAYS भारत सरकार Government of India | Mahindra Truck and Bus

ISBN 978-93-88241-38-0

This edition first published in 2018

Printed and bound in India by Manipal Technologies Limited, Manipal

This is a work of fiction. Names, characters,
places and incidents are either the product of the authors' imagination,
or are used fictitiously, and any resemblance to any actual person,
living or dead, events or locales is entirely coincidental.

Contents

Foreword

As I have mentioned elsewhere before, I have been a victim of a near-fatal road accident which kept me bed-ridden for nearly a year. This was a life-altering event for me, as it changed my perspective towards life in several ways. The accident sensitised me to the issue of road safety.

When I became the Minister for Road Transport, I realised it was a god-sent opportunity to make a difference to the road safety scenario in the country. And hence, I started espousing road safety initiatives with a new zeal.

Now, many road accidents in our country, especially the ones which result in fatalities, take place on highways. Most of these accidents involve truck drivers.

There are several reasons for these accidents: lack of training, lack of sleep, drunken driving, vision defects like cataract, and in some cases black-spots.

The government has undertaken massive drivers' training initiatives. We have supported regular health and eye check-ups of drivers. However, I have always maintained that road safety has a strong emotive angle as it puts the future of families at stake. And hence, unless the messaging extends beyond the individual and involves family members, optimal results will not be achieved.

This is why I found the #ComeHomePapa initiative fresh and unique.

To have the daughters of truck drivers contribute stories and anecdotes, which carry the message of road safety, was an excellent idea and deserves full support. In addition to road safety, it deftly weaves the issues of education of the girl child and women's empowerment into it, as well.

I have been through some of the stories. I must say they are impressive and would inspire other inventive campaigns in the future.

In India, more than seventy-five percent of road accidents happen due to human error or carelessness. While the government has taken several steps such as doubling of the total length of national highways, reducing the threshold for four-laning of highways, etc., ultimately the desired results cannot be achieved in the absence of responsible road usage. And responsible road usage at times needs to be encouraged by family members.

I congratulate Mahindra Trucks and Buses Ltd. and Tell Me Your Story for the wonderful execution of this project. I am confident that this project will inspire more such innovative initiatives on road safety where the messaging involves family members and reaches a far wider audience than what we have managed so far.

Nitin Gadkari
Minister for Road Transport, Highways, Shipping,
Water Resources and Ganga Rejuvenation

A Special Message from Mr Anand Mahindra

This is a very imaginative and valuable initiative and I am delighted to write this foreword for the first ever book of stories on road safety by daughters of truck drivers. The sentiments expressed in these stories send out the message better than any number of speeches and lectures on road safety.

The issue of road safety in our country needs to be addressed in every way possible. All of us have a stake in road safety, for ourselves and our dear ones, and we cannot leave it to be addressed by the government only. While aspects like driver education, stricter licensing, better road engineering, better signages, and more effective speed enforcement are in the hands of various regulatory and enforcement authorities, there is still a significant aspect of personal commitment, influencing of social behaviours and informal education to which we can all contribute. Each and every one of us has to be involved in making our roads safer for all of us.

This splendid initiative by Mahindra Truck and Bus Division is a reiteration of the Mahindra Group's commitment to the education and upliftment of the girl child. The roots of this book lie in the Mahindra Saarthi Abhiyaan Scholarship scheme that has awarded over a thousand scholarships to daughters of truck drivers every year since 2014. Mahindra Truck and Bus has been engaging with these girls continuously. Getting them to write on the subject of road safety is definitely a very innovative approach that resonates strongly in this age of social media.

As the father of two girls, I am aware of the special bond that exists between a father and his daughter, and the concern she would feel for his wellbeing, especially if her father is a truck driver. This little book is a wonderful testimony to the fears and hopes, the joys and sorrows, and above all, the deep connection between these girls and their fathers.

I wish you happy reading! The next time you are on the road, please spare a thought for these fathers and their daughters eagerly waiting for them at home!

Anand Mahindra
Chairman, Mahindra Group

Introduction

Koral Dasgupta

The softest touch is always the dearest memory. Memories nurture relationships. And relationships are the genesis of a generation.

#ComeHomePapa is not only a collection of short stories that connect authors to the audience, but stories that will help build relationships between socially and economically disparate sectors, bridging the gaps with common emotions. Emotions that bind fathers and daughters, irrespective of class, caste, creed, religion. Emotion that makes you take a closer look at the coin from the other side.

While driving on the roads, when you are impatient to leave behind that path-blocking truck in front, getting irritated if you don't get a pass, have you ever tried to look at the driver of that truck? Perhaps you haven't. Because the truck driver doesn't feature anywhere close to your world. But then, is that true?

You shop for items you regularly need from stores, be it rice or bricks or clothes. The stores maintain an inventory to service customers like you. This inventory is delivered to them and other stores like them, by trucks, That's how truck drivers cater to our needs without our knowledge.

What is your impression of a truck driver, may I ask? A shabbily dressed, scruffy-looking man? An alcoholic? An illiterate, uncouth guy? Or one of the culprits accused in accident cases pending in the court? The unknown face behind the steering wheel of a heavy vehicle who just needs to get out of your way?

You probably haven't ever thought of these men as *fathers*, waiting to return to their children at the end of a hard day, just like we all do. Unlike us though, they don't get to go home every day, as consignments take them to far-off places, keeping them away from their families for days or even months.

Truck drivers are soldiers dedicated to the smooth running of the buyer-consumer economy and yet, the worst sufferers of the system. They have to drive in extreme conditions if required and bear many hardships on the road, for very little money. They are often stripped of their self-respect for any mistake, without ascertaining whether they are responsible for it or not. They are most vulnerable to road accidents as they spend so much time on the roads. They are the victims of dacoity, robberies and ambushes. They have to contend with the vagaries of the weather and the unfamiliarity of the terrain. And all the while, their families live under great stress, praying for their safety.

It hasn't occurred to many of us, I am sure, that these truck drivers may be fathers to daughters who are aspiring or qualified doctors, engineers, architects, IAS officers or MBAs. Well, the #ComeHomePapa initiative by Mahindra Truck and Bus in collaboration with #TellMeYourStory, introduces us, through the voices of these daughters, to the reality of the hardships and hazards of their fathers' tireless journeys.

Come Home, Papa is a collection of such stories where fathers dream and work hard to get their daughters educated and well placed; where the daughters with their education, vision and ability are now analysing their fathers' lives and reaching out to more people to seek better working conditions, fair treatment and justice for all truck drivers. The kind of justice which cannot be enforced by a mere court of law, but only by the empathy of fellow human beings.

The #ComeHomePapa initiative would like to create this awareness in the hope that the next time we see a huge truck lumbering ahead of us, not allowing us to pass, we see the driver of the truck as a father, husband, son... and show him some patience and kindness.

I wholeheartedly thank the support of the Ministry of Road Transport and Highways as well as Mahindra Truck and Bus, for hosting this ambitious project and for extending their assistance and backing for its smooth execution, at every level. The cooperation we have received from the Mahindra team, especially from Mr Rajeev Malik and Mr Atin Moulik, has been phenomenal. We, the team of #TellMeYourStory, have taken back immense learning from the project.

The vision of #TellMeYourStory has been to encourage unheard voices and inspire them to come out with hitherto untold stories. #ComeHomePapa is one such initiative. It explores stories of road robbery and road rage, of facing natural calamities and financial struggles, of accidents and precautions, very much from the grass-root level. Such rigorous, unpretentious expressions of experiences on the road, laced with a daughter's concerns for her father, do not come to light everyday. We have also made a conscious decision to retain the original tone and raw intensity of the stories. That is why we decided to stick to minimal editing. By doing so, we have tried our level best to preserve the style and language used by each of our bright and passionate writers in this collection of stories. We cherish each of their accounts and hope that they will be instrumental in generating awareness about road safety. We also hope that more people from less privileged groups will be encouraged to dream big, with the assurance that with education, their children will have a better life and a better future.

The #ComeHomePapa project has introduced to us another social sector from a whole new perspective; working on it has helped us to engage with talent from across India. On the one hand we had ace professionals joining us; on the other, the project gave us the chance to extend work opportunities to home-makers, senior citizens and students—people who are qualified but for some reason unavailable for full-time employment.

My special thanks to the #TellMeYourStory community for the relationships that were forged and personal growth that we have experienced in the span of a little over a year since we started our operations. We wouldn't have been what we are without our authors and readers.

I thank our esteemed jury for the project—Kiran Manral, Dr Kheya Baidya and Raj K. Mitra—for reading the touching stories and helping us select the winning entries which are to be awarded and/or included in the book. Thanks to Dr Avani Desai and Shelly Bhoil for standing by us.

Thanks to Aarefa Faridoon, Dr Anindita Chatterjee, Anusuya Suresh, Bhavi Gathani, Gaurav Sharma Lakhi, Harshal Desai, Insha Faridoon, Joel Guha, Kanchana Banerjee, Kanishk Sharma, Kathakali Mukherjee, Meera Srikanth, Nazneen Kachwala, Nitya Kannan, Roshni

Vijay, Rumi Dasgupta, Sharmistha Ghosal, Sufia Khatoon, Vani Kaushal, Swanand Kulkarni and Varsha Prasad for taking over the immense work, at various editorial and administrative levels.

Many thanks to Amaryllis, an Imprint of Manjul Publishing House for taking the project ahead with us and bringing out a beautiful anthology of short stories. It has been a great pleasure working with Rashmi Menon, Keerti Ramachandra and Megha Parmar.

Having walked a long path, it is now time for us to step back and let the readers take over.

I would like all our readers to know that a part of the proceeds received from the sale of each copy of Come Home, Papa *will go into the welfare and education of many more daughters of truck drivers.*

Hope you enjoy reading this book as much as we have cherished curating it.

Koral Dasgupta
Founder of www.tellmeyourstory.in

1

My Papa

Bersha Kumari

My father is a truck driver and I am very proud to be a truck driver's daughter.

Papa has been driving a truck for the past thirty years and so far, by God's grace there have been no accidents in his career because he knows that his life is connected with four others. Papa has spent all his life making a thousand sacrifices silently and struggled to ensure that no discomfort touches his family. He says he doesn't feel bad that he didn't save much money, because it went into the education of his daughters.

We realise that and so we study well because it makes him happy. He feels proud whenever our photographs or our achievements are reported in newspapers or any other media, and shows them to his friends and colleagues with teary eyes. We also try to keep him free from tension when he is at home. So if we are in any sort of difficulty we try to hide it from him.

When he comes home, we—my two brothers, my

sister and I—ensure that we are always around him and there for him so that he never feels lonely in his life and in his journey as well.

To show him how much we care about him and to keep us always in his mind, we have placed a family photograph in his truck.

Every time he comes home, Papa has many stories to tell—of some new adventure, a new incident, interesting people he met and so many more fascinating things.

Some stories tell what real life is. Many are sad, incredible and inspirational, and a few of them perfectly express the love we feel for that special someone who has stood by us all his life. In my story, this 'someone' is none other than my father.

There are lessons which I can't learn in any college or class lecture. Looking at his journey, one thing I have come to know about life is that it is full of ups and downs. Every time he is back home after finishing a difficult task, our confidence levels increase.

Three years back I was in college and my semester exams were going on. My younger sister was about to go to Kota for her IIT preparation. For her admission my father had to arrange a huge sum of money. There were only two days left for her to leave, but Papa hadn't been able to gather the complete amount. So he took a driving assignment which was offering him almost double of the usual amount. Despite being unwell he went ahead for work. Before leaving the house he told my younger sister not to worry and that he will be back in time. He did not tell anyone about his sickness. He thought that it would bring my sister's morale down when she was about to start a new phase in her life.

My father is diabetic. In the middle of the journey, suddenly his sugar levels decreased to below normal and he fainted while driving. By God's grace he had a companion in the truck, who took care of him and later called my uncle to inform us. That day my father was saved from a major accident. It was midnight. Everyone was sleeping at home, unaware of the incident. My father was admitted to a nearby hospital called LIFE. At one past midnight my mother received a call. For a moment, she seemed as though she were not in her senses and went completely blank. At that time I couldn't understand what to do. But after gathering her composure, she took out the money my father had kept for my sister's admission and went to the hospital. He was in the emergency ward. No one was allowed to meet him. When he regained consciousness he met everyone and told my sister not to lose faith as we still had time.

His smiling face hid all his pain. I must say that my father had seen death very closely. My father always says, 'Don't lose the courage to face troubles. Let them come and go, but don't step back.'

The ghosts of this incident still chase us. If my father doesn't come back home in time, my mother's face goes pale while waiting for him. Many times we are unable to contact him as he would be driving in remote areas with bad network. We spend sleepless nights waiting for him and when he returns we heave a sigh of relief.

One day I will make every dream of my father come true. Keeping that in mind, I work hard. I am an intern with Tech Mahindra now. The way my father and Tech Mahindra are helping me in my studies, I believe that one day I will achieve what my father wants from me. Tech Mahindra has supported me and my father so much that I want to serve this organisation as a software engineer, which would be the greatest gift I can give to my father, and also to this organisation.

2

A Winter's Tale

Bulbul Khan and Rukhasar Khan

We were going to Mathura from our hometown, Kharmani Village. Father was driving a Bolero and we were sitting next to him. He was driving at a speed of approximately sixty kilometres per hour. He did not have the seat belt on. We reminded him to strap it on but he said he would do so later, at Goverdhan Churaya.

As we neared Kolapur, a girl riding her scooty suddenly crossed the road from the opposite side and came right in front our vehicle. Father applied the emergency brake. Due to this sudden action he was thrown forward and he crashed into the steering wheel of the Bolero. He was badly hurt by the impact. Somehow, we managed to reach Mathura. The next day, Father developed severe chest pain, so he had to go to a doctor. After many medical check-ups and a lot of medicines, Father recovered. It took nearly twenty-one days for him to feel better. We, too, underwent trauma, watching him go through this ordeal. We kept feeling bad that we hadn't forced him enough to wear the seat belt. We should not have let him postpone this simple act. Because, as you can see, road accidents don't always happen due to the driver's negligence. They often take place when someone else on the road isn't as responsible with his or her vehicle. It's wiser to use the safety aids rather than ignore them and suffer.

I would like to share another example of something happening when it is not your fault. Father had loaded his Maxi pick-up vehicle with marble slabs and tiles and was driving to deliver the goods. It was 8 o'clock at night and there were no street lights. He did not see the speed breaker on the road. It was much higher than normal, but he had missed it in the dim light. His vehicle jumped over it and landed with a big thud. Due to the severe jolt the marble slabs broke. Father realised that the entire load was damaged. It was such an unnecessary waste of money and effort. But there was nothing anyone could do. There was no point in crying over spilt milk! This is a matter for the authorities to take note of. When roads are not well-lit, even the slightest mistake can wreak havoc. Also speed breakers of such height are dangerous for all vehicles, especially two-wheelers. During the winter months when dense fog reduces visibility greatly, driving becomes even more risky.

We have had personal experience of that too.

My mother, sister, uncle and I had gone to Aligarh,

some seventy kilometres from our home. Father was driving his Bolero. We started our journey in the afternoon and reached Aligarh around 5 o'clock in the evening. Leaving us with our aunt's family, he and Uncle went to the transport company to collect some materials which had to be dropped off at Mathura. They were told to come back and load the Bolero truck after dinner. The materials were to be delivered by 7 o'clock the next morning.

Father and Uncle joined us around 8 p.m. and we all had dinner. He instructed us to sleep early as we would be starting at 4 a.m. to reach Mathura by 6.30 a.m. He then went back to load the truck. We woke up early in the morning, as planned, had tea and left. When we reached the highway, the fog was so dense that we couldn't see beyond two metres.

It would be very dangerous to make any progress with a heavy vehicle under such conditions. How would we reach the destination on time? All of us were very scared. Since Father had to deliver the goods by 7 a.m. under any circumstances, we had no choice but to carry on. Uncle decided to walk in front of the truck so that Father could drive slowly behind him! We all took turns to lead the way while Father followed. Finally by 8 o'clock the fog began to lift. We managed to reach our destination at 10.30 a.m. The person who received the materials deducted ₹500 from Father's payment for coming late!

Ever since then, before Father goes out on long-distance driving jobs, we check the weather conditions religiously either on the internet, the television or the newspapers, or just force him to speak to a local person at the destination so that he is prepared for the ordeal, if any.

3

Lessons of the Road

Maganti Lavanya

My father has been a truck driver for the past fifteen years. He is a very organised person who always keeps safety as his top priority. He is particular about his vehicle's maintenance and before starting a long journey he double checks to make sure that his vehicle is in good condition. He tries to get enough rest so that he can concentrate on the road while driving. He would never violate the speed limits set by the authorities under any circumstances. He is alert to the unexpected obstacles that can come in his way, like the vehicle in front stopping suddenly without warning, or a motorist overtaking from the wrong side, or another vehicle cutting into the main road from a side lane. Many drivers are careless about taking a diversion—they turn without switching on their indicator lights and that can be very dangerous. In case of traffic jams, he waits patiently for the traffic to clear instead of rushing into by lanes and restricted roads, which are not meant for public use. Also, my father plans his travel in advance, based on the area he will be driving through. This way he can pass through forest areas during the daytime, minimising chances of road robbery, or attacks by wild animals, or getting stuck in a lonely deserted area in case of a breakdown.

In spite of being so systematic, unpredictable dangers lurk in the lives of truck drivers. Father often shares experiences from his life and the lives of his driver friends. They sometimes send a chill down my spine.

Here is one such story.

It was raining heavily. This friend of my father's did not pay attention to the warnings and went ahead with his vehicle through the flooded area, putting his life at risk. After a certain point, the flow of the water was such that the movement of the truck was beyond human control. The truck was washed off the bridge. To ensure his own safety, the driver jumped out of the window of the truck thinking he would swim ashore. But the currents were so strong that he could have been swept away.

However, he had the presence of mind to catch hold of the branch of a tree, which was three-fourths submerged in the flood water. The driver held on to the branch tightly while the gushing water flowed past him. There was no way he could move to either shore. For more than six hours he was stuck there until the rescue team arrived, and with the help of the local villagers, they used ropes to pull him out. The driver had made an unwise decision by going against the rules, ignoring all the warnings. He had foolishly over-estimated his strength, not realising the colossal force of nature. However, his presence of mind and the smart move to hold on to the branch of the tree and wait to get rescued was a brave act.

Even if you are stuck in a difficult situation, presence of mind helps you take the right decision and steer you out of trouble. That is the lesson you must learn from this story, my father used to say. My father firmly believes that some people overspeed on the roads for the pure thrill it gives them, for excitement and fun. They do not stop to think about the consequences of their actions. To explain the dangers of over-speeding, he told us this story of a truck driver who was speeding on the highway. He was taken by surprise when an auto rickshaw wheeled into his path through a sharp cut in the road. The truck driver tried to avoid collision by applying sudden brakes and making an abrupt turn. Because of this the truck overturned. Fortunately, the driver escaped without any injuries. But the carelessness of the driver could have resulted in a huge crash and left the vehicle badly damaged.

My father is an easygoing person and never gets into trouble with fellow drivers or the local people of the area he is driving through. Also, he will never get into silly speeding challenges like overtaking a bus or a truck at high speed, jeopardising his own life and the lives of others. He is particular about keeping in touch with the family when he is away on long trips.

My sister and I always stay connected with him. He calls us when he is resting during his journeys. We have been instructed to leave a missed call in case we need to talk to him. He calls us as soon as he gets to stop somewhere. That is because Father never uses his cell phone when he is driving. He keeps warning my sister and me of the perils of speaking on the cell phone while driving. Sometimes when he is not reachable by phone for a long time, my sister and I get very anxious. At such times our mother tells us to be strong and not panic as Father might be passing through an area with no network coverage.

Every time Father goes on a long trip he lets us know the day he will be returning because he knows my sister and I will be waiting eagerly for him to come home. And he never forgets to inform us if he is stuck somewhere and is delayed. Otherwise, we will all worry, he knows.

It gets difficult sometimes but we have now grown up with these uncertainties. My father may not be equipped with formal degrees, but the road has taught him all kinds of valuable life lessons. We are lucky to have him share these lessons with us.

4

Yield The Right Of Way

Anujna Suvarna

Two years ago, my father had a very scary experience while driving. His job is to drive an eighteen-wheel truck, which carries huge containers that come by sea to the port depots and then are delivered to many inland destinations. That day Father was transporting goods to a faraway place in his truck. As he was driving along a busy road, he saw a small Maruti Zen behind his vehicle. Since there was heavy traffic ahead he couldn't make way for the car to overtake him.

After three kilometres or so the road became a single-lane road. My father had to drive on the right side. He was driving slowly as the truck was heavily loaded. A little while later he felt some kind of friction which was slowing down the vehicle more and more. There was also the smell of burning rubber. He pulled over to the side and stopped the truck to inspect the vehicle. He walked to the back of the truck to check whether the brake pipe was loose. But there was no such problem. He came to the front to see if anything was wrong there. That's when he got the shock of his life. The Maruti Zen, which was trying to overtake him three kilometres back, was under his vehicle! It was as if someone had attached the car to his truck. For about twenty feet his heavy vehicle had driven with the car tucked under it!

With his heart beating fast and hands trembling, my father opened the car door on the left side. There was an eighty-year-old lady and a younger man, her son, in the car. Father slowly helped them get out. They looked pale and terrified, as though they had lost all hopes of coming out alive. Fortunately, no harm had come to them. When they realised that they were safe, they were relieved enough to talk. They told my father that they were returning home from the temple at Kollur. God had protected them. But the car was damaged badly and was completely out of shape.

When I first heard the story I asked my father, 'But, Papa, how is it you didn't hear anything? How is it you didn't see the car?'

'Trailer vehicles have powerful air conditioners in them, due to which one cannot hear any noise from outside,' my father answered. 'Also, the dashboard in front of the driver's seat is at a height. So I couldn't see that small vehicle in front either.'

But my father was badly shaken. He felt that he had almost killed two people. He remembers this incident many a time. Every time he narrates it, I can see the pain on his face. In the twenty-eight years that he has been driving, this was the first unpleasant experience he had had.

My father is a responsible truck driver. No accident has ever taken place due to his carelessness, primarily because he values life. Whenever he drives, he makes sure enough distance is maintained between his vehicle and other vehicles.

He always applies the 'safety first' rule in his life and encourages us to follow the same in our lives too. He tells us, 'Also pray for the family members and friends of our neighbour drivers to be safe. It is important for us to keep that in mind.'

It is always better to take precautions and maintain safety standards, especially when driving. I wish our education system will include lectures on road safety because we see so many youngsters losing their lives on the roads as they do not observe traffic rules and safety guidelines. Either because they are ignorant of them or are careless and choose to ignore them. It is the duty of every citizen to create awareness and prevent blood being shed on the roads.

Like my father's motto, mine is also 'Yield the right of way'.

5

Safety of Drivers

Sonali Dyaneshwar Jamadar

I am in an awe of my father. He is my idol, the centre of my faith. He is an uneducated man; perhaps that's why he decided to give me the best education possible despite our limited economic resources. We do not have any property, neither a house, nor a bank balance. We live in a rented house. We meet the household expenses with whatever my father earns working for others. And it's not easy, for sometimes we have to manage with very little money. What we lack in money my father makes up with love. He is like the rain-bearing cloud pouring affection on my mother and me.

To provide for us, my father, who is a truck driver, works tirelessly. He has no time for himself. His is a harsh life where he faces many hardships, including not having time to eat a morsel of food because he has to reach somewhere at a particular time. He often drives during the day and through the night. Why does he work so hard? So that we are able to live comfortably and are not deprived of anything. I know he suffers immensely, but he never lets us feel his pain. It is so inspiring to see him do his job honestly, without complaint.

Just as most children's fathers return home at night, I feel that my father too should come home, that I should be able to see him every day. But he is always travelling, and spends not more than two to three days at home with us. Circumstances are such that he has to stay away from us for long. So when he comes back home we celebrate almost as if it is Diwali. We spend all our time in his company and rejoice that he has come home safely. When my father is away from home I miss him terribly. I comfort myself by looking at his photograph and praying for him to return home safely.

To give you an example of the kind of dangers a truck driver faces, I would like to tell this story. This incident pulled the ground from under my feet. That day as I was getting ready to go to college my father gave me ₹200 and assured me that he would give me more the next time. Hardly had he left for work when we got a phone call from someone saying Father had met with an accident close to the house. I was badly shaken. With tears rolling down my cheeks, I immediately rushed to the site of the accident along with my mother. We were shocked to see Father had suffered serious injuries to his hands and his head. His clothes were stained with blood and he was moaning in pain. Luckily, there was a hospital nearby but they refused to treat him as they were not equipped to do so. We had to shift him to another hospital where he was admitted in the ICU. Father responded well to the treatment and his condition improved after three-four days. Thanks to the timely intervention of the doctors, my father got a new lease of life. It was nothing short of a rebirth. We had no money to pay the hospital bills so we borrowed money and even went without food.

It was later I came to know that a four-wheeler coming from the opposite direction had knocked down my father. When we reported the accident to the police, they assured us that an investigation would be conducted and action taken against the car driver. But the very next day, the police said the matter should be settled by accepting ₹20,000 from the car driver. We haven't received even one rupee till date. The police had closed the case so we got neither any assistance nor justice. That day I learnt that the poor have no voice. Most of the time it is because they are not educated and are not aware of the law or do not know what rights they have. Also, they do not have the confidence to fight for themselves.

Though I am educated, at that time I felt it was more prudent to take care of my father's health rather than take legal action. The injury suffered by my father in this accident still raises its head from time to time, causing him great pain, but he has to continue working. There is no alternative before him.

Another incident which shows how unsafe and risky a driver's life is took place recently, just three to four months back. My father had gone to Jamshedpur, and since it was his first time there, he did not know anything about the topography of the area. While negotiating a turn in the difficult terrains of Jharkhand, his vehicle broke down. It was essential to repair the truck in order to move ahead. But since it was night and in the middle of a lonely, forested area, he couldn't get any assistance. Nor could he leave the truck and go looking for help. He had no choice but to wait for daybreak before any help arrived. Somehow he gathered the courage to face the situation. He remained seated inside the vehicle, chanting his prayers and sometime later, fell asleep. Around 1 or 2 o'clock at night, he was rudely awakened by a sound. He wondered what it was but before he could find out, a gang of robbers attacked him. They beat him black and blue, snatched his mobile, took away the ₹15,000 he was carrying and the diesel from the truck, and left him there to perish. Thankfully he survived. You cannot even imagine how terrible things could have been.

Though my father never complains I wish there was some arrangement to ensure the safety of drivers. Transport company owners who employ drivers, the police and the government should work together to make roads, especially highways, safe for truck drivers who usually drive at night, mostly alone, often through dangerous territories. I think it is because of the hardships that my father has faced, that he emphasizes on the importance of my education. I also truly believe that it is education that makes a person a responsible citizen. Education can help one realise one's full potential, bring about the development of one's inherent qualities, lead youth in the right direction and uplift society by making us all ideal citizens. As my father insists, without education, human life is worthless.

6

Don't Drink and Drive

T. Sivasri

The incident happened in 2006 and it is true.

My uncle used to drive a goods auto that he had hired. The income from that was sufficient for him. However, after he got married, he realised he wasn't making enough from the rented auto, and so he decided to buy his own auto on instalments. It seemed like an excellent decision as by that time my uncle had a daughter. Keeping the girl's future in mind, he and my aunt went ahead with their plans. They sold whatever jewellery they had and purchased a new goods auto, happy that they now had their own vehicle.

But that happiness lasted only a few months.

My uncle, who was just twenty-eight years old, died in a major road accident, leaving my aunt and my little cousin behind.

My uncle hailed from Pammal near Pallavaram in Chennai. It was his daily routine to go to Kanchipuram in the evening, load the auto and bring back the goods to Tambaram the next morning. On the evening of 9 September, he took leave of his wife and daughter as usual, little knowing that it would be the last time he would see them. As the auto was empty on the way to Kanchipuram, he took a friend of his and a few passengers along. The friend was in the passenger seat, the others seated in the rear and my uncle was driving. As they approached Adancheri, the auto collided with a minibus that was going in the opposite direction, from Vandalur to Vellore. In that split second of the impact, my uncle pushed his friend out of the vehicle. He escaped with head injuries. Some of the passengers were thrown out too, and they were saved. Not my uncle, though. His auto was smashed and he died on the spot. Even as he took his last breath, he kept repeating his daughter's name.

That day, my aunt lost her husband, and my cousin, who was not even a year old, became fatherless. My uncle wanted to have a grand celebration for her first birthday but that wasn't to be. His dream of seeing his daughter become a doctor will also remain unfulfilled.

What was more shocking for us than the news of my uncle's death was the fact that he had died because the minibus driver was drunk and overspeeding. He lost control and crashed into the auto. We will never see my uncle again, but not a day goes by when we don't remember him and think that perhaps the accident wouldn't have happened if the minibus driver was not under the influence of alcohol that day.

This one incident deeply affected our lives because my father is a driver too. A truck driver. His experiences in life have taught me a lot, but one lesson that stands out distinctly is this: When we drive we should do so with total alertness. Safe and good driving demands that a driver must never drive after drinking alcohol. He must make sure he is not too tired or sleepy when at the wheel. Nor should he undertake a long drive when he is under any kind of stress.

A driver is the head of the family, a father to his children, a husband to his wife, a son to his parents, a brother to his siblings. One wrong decision on his part, and it is the entire family that suffers.

Mistakes can cost dearly and one might have to pay for them with one's life. We have seen that in my family and I know how much it hurts. I wish that the incident that happened with my uncle should not happen to anyone else. You can achieve everything, but nothing can compensate for the loss of a human life.

7

Road Rage

Shahanaj Parveen

Truck drivers sometimes end up suffering for no fault of theirs, and my father, who has been driving a truck since 1986, is no exception. He has had to face great hardships. Many of his stories are truly horrifying.

It was 1998. My father was driving his vehicle. Suddenly, a young school student on a bicycle with a man sitting on the carrier seat collided with the truck. As a result, the man sitting on the carrier seat died on the spot. My father was arrested and put in jail for two days. A case was filed against him which dragged on for ten years. He had to appear before the court every month. We had to spend a lot of money for his appearances in court and soon we were in a very difficult financial position.

Many times, my father has to drive on roads that are so unnavigable that they invite major accidents. At some places, there are no speed breakers. Many roads have such deep potholes that when it rains heavily, they fill up with so much water that people can drown in them. Such potholes have caused so many accidents too, but the administration pays no attention to any complaints. Kordha T.P. Nagar is one such place where accidents occur almost daily. As for the roads leading to the mines, they are so bad that most vehicles get stranded there for two or three days. If that was not enough, the moment they come out, they face road blockades on a regular basis.

Once, my father was driving through a particularly notorious village. Suddenly the village people stopped his vehicle and started beating him with slippers and sticks. They broke the windscreen and the windows of his vehicle and snatched the money he was carrying. Since he was alone he was helpless and could do nothing. Thereafter he lodged a report at the police station and all those men were caught.

Another time in 2008, my father was returning from Raipur after unloading all the goods there. Some bandits attacked him. They sprayed something on him that made him unconscious and stole his money and licence. My father had to get another licence made.

Once, when he was sleeping inside his vehicle in Ratanpur, someone stole the battery and diesel from his vehicle. My father had to pay for all that though it was not his fault.

Recently, my father and his friends, who are also drivers, were crossing a railway line, when eight-ten goons riding on bikes encircled them and started beating and looting them. One of the drivers escaped from there and went straight to the police station to get an F.I.R. lodged. The police reached the spot quickly, and saw how these goons had beaten one of the drivers. Some of the goondas were arrested but many of them fled. During interrogation, it came to light that many of the goons belonged to well-to-do, educated families. Thankfully, the police took harsh measures against all of them.

Another time, my father's boss wanted the goods from my father's vehicle to be transferred to another vehicle. As my father was doing this some policemen present near the petrol pump took action against him. They arrested him and kept him in custody. For three days he was in the lock-up. They assumed he was attempting a theft. If only they had checked with the owner and believed my father's explanation! A misunderstanding had cost him three days inside the jail.

My father tells me that he cannot get a wink of sleep at night, especially when his vehicle breaks down. At times he has had to spend nights all alone in jungles with wild animals. But his toughest experiences have been those when he has had to travel through areas that are notorious for thrashing, looting and attacking poor drivers.

There have been times when my father has not been able to reach in time to attend the last rites of members of our family. This makes him feel very bad.

But Father says that since he must continue to drive, he ignores all these hazards and concentrates on driving.

Needless to say, this is why we all worry so much about my father when he does not return home in time. All day, our eyes remain fixed on the door. We wonder whether he is okay or whether he has taken his food on time or whether he would have managed to get some rest. We fervently hope his vehicle hasn't had a breakdown. It is hard to imagine how he manages in spite of all these difficulties

Honestly, all I want to do is settle myself financially and socially as soon as possible and extend whatever help I can to my father.

8

That Diwali

Ramija Abdulgafar Shirgruppe

How would you feel if your father is falsely accused of killing someone, someone who probably invited his own death by driving under the influence of alcohol?

This is the story of what happened to my father. As a truck driver he endures a lot of hardships related to his work, but if he is punished for no fault of his, it seems very unfair and unjust.

I come from an ordinary family that consists of my parents, brothers and sisters and of course me. My father is a truck driver and he has been driving for almost twenty years. Even then we worry about him, not knowing whether we are going to see him again, more so when he drives at night or goes far away from home. We just pray to God that everything should be okay and that God be merciful to my father.

When I was in the eighth grade an incident took place, which none of us have forgotten. My father used to go to far off places to procure sand. He usually went alone, and never had another driver or assistant with him. It was Diwali, the day when people light lamps in their houses to celebrate the festival but the lamps in our house were put out that day.

While my father was driving his truck, he noticed a man on a two-wheeler behind him. The man was drunk and driving very fast. Suddenly the two-wheeler crashed into the truck. The man suffered head injuries and died on the spot. All this was seen by a person standing close by.

Usually when something like this happens, the public does not see whose fault it is and only beats up the truck driver. However, in this case, there was an eye-witness, and he was kind to my father who was badly shaken by the accident. It had never happened to him before. The man gave my father a glass of water and some tea and waited there until the police arrived. At around 6 p.m. we got a call from my father telling us about the accident and that the police had arrested him. Before he could say anything more his mobile got disconnected. We felt something bad had happened to my father. All of us were in a terrible state, especially my mother who could not stop crying. We all felt that my father had left us.

A short while later, the truck owner came to our house and told us what had happened. My father was proved innocent as the medical check-up proved that the person who died had nintey percent alcohol in his blood, whereas my father had none. Although my father had been proved innocent, he had to spend two days at the police station.

Every time he goes out to work we ask him one question: 'When will you be back home?' And until he comes home we pray for his safety.

It is my sincere request to all drivers of all vehicles not to drive under the influence of alcohol, or use a mobile phone while driving. Remember, someone is waiting for you back home.

9

Victim of Child Abuse

Riya Dahiya

As the eldest child and the only daughter among my siblings, I am fortunate to be very close to my father. But being the eldest also means that I started shouldering his responsibilities at a very young age.

My father is a truck driver and he runs his vehicle on the roads of Hissar, Faridabad, Gurgaon and Karnal. Usually he goes on a trip for five to ten days. Whenever he goes for a long trip he prepares us in advance. All the major household tasks are taken care of by him before he sets out on a new trip of uncertainty; his homecoming brings with it lots of stories told to us over a meal.

All my childhood days were spent waiting for my father. The happiness of seeing him after a long time as well as his travel stories had become an integral part of our life. Through these tales I learned that my dad's life is full of danger because of the nature of his job, but we now know how to live with the uncertainty. I secretly pray for my dad's safety and for him to be able to come home to us. In his absence I learnt to take care of my family. I became more responsible during my teenage years.

One night I was waiting eagerly for my father because I had some good news to announce to him. The most-awaited class XII results had come out and I had done well after putting in a lot of hard work and going through great hardships. But he did not come; none of our calls could get through to him as his phone was not reachable, and then it got switched off. We had no option but to wait and pray for his wellbeing and that's what we did for the next three days. The morning after three sleepless nights finally turned out to be a 'good morning' for us. The doorbell rang at 4 a.m. We were awake and ran to the door immediately. We could not believe that he was back. It took us all a few hours to get back to normal and then what he narrated to us came as the biggest shock, especially for me.

On his trip to Muzaffarnagar, Father had stopped for dinner just after crossing Shamli. He would be driving for the whole night after that. As soon as he started another night's journey, he was stopped by the patrol police and while checking the truck, they found a little girl hidden behind the cycle parts that were being transported. My father was as shocked to see the girl as we were on hearing about it. Innumerable thoughts ran through our minds at once.

The police seized the truck and took the little girl and my father into custody. The thought of our father being caught by the police and then being jailed brought tears to our eyes.

An investigation at the station followed. Our hearts skipped a beat when my father told us what came out of it. The little girl, named Trisha, was a victim of child abuse and out of fear she had hidden in the loaded truck to escape from the clutches of one of her neighbours—an 'uncle' who had been abusing her after her mother's death. Trisha's father worked somewhere in Delhi and used to send money to her uncle, whom he trusted blindly, to look after his little daughter. My father, rather than breathing a sigh of relief on being acquitted by the police, decided to help Trisha reunite with her dad, while the police did their job simultaneously.

After successfully handing over Trisha to her dad, he came back home and taught us the most important lesson of our lives—to be humane, to be kind and to raise our voice against exploitation.

10

That Fateful Night

Priti Chaudhary

Once in 2013, my father was driving his truck late at night in chilly winter weather. It was the month of December and there was a thick fog, so Father drove to the side of the road and decided to halt there since visibility was low. A few other truck drivers, who were travelling along the same route, also waited there till the fog cleared. All of them went to sleep. A little after midnight my father smelt smoke and woke up. He was shocked to see that his vehicle had caught fire.

He panicked when he saw fire all around. He tried to open the vehicle from inside, but the door would not open. He tried to break the glass but in the confusion, he could not do so. The fire started spreading quickly and appeared to get more dangerous by the second. Luckily my father suddenly came to his senses. He grabbed the vehicle's papers, which are very important. With great difficulty he managed to break the glass and escape through the window. Though paper burns easily, he managed to take them out intact.

God was very kind to us that day. He helped my father escape without any major harm or injury. He was admitted to the local hospital because he had fainted due to choking on smoke, and had sustained some minor injuries too. The villagers tried to put out the fire with water, but by the time the fire brigade arrived, the vehicle was entirely burnt.

We got to know about the incident several hours later, almost at dawn. When Father had tried to call from the hospital, he realised that his phone was burnt too. Someone called us and gave us this news. We immediately left for the hospital. Fortunately, he was sent home after one day. When Father described the incident to us later, we were so scared we felt the ground under our feet was shaking! Father has to face such issues daily when driving a truck, not knowing when his life will be in danger.

My father is everything to my family and me. If he is not there, there will be no happiness left. Father is an honest, hardworking, and sincere person. He has always taught us never to do anything wrong. Perhaps it is due to his good deeds that God has always saved him from misfortune.

I thank the Mahindra Company with all my heart and I am indebted to the Mahindra Saarthi Abhiyaan for this opportunity. I am very happy that Mahindra is providing new opportunities for educating the daughters of truck drivers.

11

The Sight of Death

Jiya

My father has been working as a truck driver since 1977. In those initial years, there were not many means of communication, not even mobile phones. Once he set out on a trip, we had no way of contacting him or knowing his condition till he returned home. Imagine how anxious we would all feel, especially when he used to be driving in remote terrains.

Among the many stories my father tells me, some are about road accidents. The first accident he told me about happened on the road between Lucknow and Hardoi at 8 o'clock in the morning. The truck was carrying coal, and my father's elder brother was driving the vehicle, taking it from Banaras to Hardoi. My father was also travelling in the truck. My uncle got a few passengers along the way in order to earn some more money. He made them sit in the truck which was already overloaded. While negotiating a turn, the truck overturned and one passenger got buried under the coal and died. My father was also seriously injured but he survived the accident by God's grace.

Despite sustaining serious injuries in the accident, my father and uncle kept things to themselves as there was no convenient mode for communication. Our families came to know about the accident much later as the place where the accident had taken place was about 250 kilometres away from our house. There was no telephone facility, which made it very difficult for us to reach him. We will never be able to forget that day. My prayer to God is that he lets no one suffer a similar fate.

One more accident witnessed by my father happened in 1998 when he was driving from Kanpur to Ahmedabad. A truck that was ahead of his vehicle was loaded with iron angles, girders and iron channels. A bus coming from behind overtook him at high speed and crashed into the back of the truck. The impact was so severe that the iron angles in the truck tore through the driver's cabin and pierced his chest. The driver died instantly. The window was open and the dead driver was still seated on his seat when my father saw him. He was so shaken by the accident that he ran a high temperature for several days after that.

My father wanted to give us the best education but due to our economic condition he could only educate me up to BA. All my sisters are educated too. I want to now pursue an LLB degree and support my father.

12
The Dream of a Beautiful Life

Gurdeep Kaur

In the beautiful valley of Kashmir where everything is a sign of God's love for Earth and the healing powers of nature for mankind, I live a life which is mostly unheard of and unseen. I am the daughter of a truck driver. I am proud to be one but I live in a pool of pain—one that not everyone can understand. Every day we dream of a beautiful life. The place we live in is called 'Heaven' but my father lives through hell every day. Rain, storms, floods, and everything else that makes life difficult—we can stay away from all this, but a truck driver has to keep driving, no matter what comes his way.

The life of truck drivers is not an easy one. They spend up to fourteen hours a day driving and battling severe road conditions. My father has to drive through hills, narrow roads, heavy rain, landslides, and sometimes things one can never foresee or imagine. They have to be constantly alert and drive efficiently and carefully, for the safety of themselves as well as everyone else on the road.

Drivers have to be very attentive, and always keep an eye on the road, looking to the left, right, front, and back simultaneously so they can avoid any possible mishap. Their biggest concern are those drivers who overtake, take a turn without warning, pull up suddenly especially while driving uphill, or slow down abruptly. This kind of road behaviour can cause fatal accidents resulting in the loss of precious lives. Unfortunately, people do not realise the pain that drivers go through every day.

For some of us, it might sound like a normal incident where a life-threatening situation looks us in the face and we must decide whether we can react and live to tell the tale. Many would perish at the thought of this, others might laugh it out, a few might think that it's all in a day's work, but to my father it isn't so. He works day and night, always driving, always risking his life to give his family a beautiful life. It's not that easy to be so selfless and think about the value of life. I think it's rightly said that only those who have tasted loss can understand the true value of things. Life too is such a fragile and valuable thing.

My father was travelling to Srinagar one foggy night on the very narrow and steep roads of Kashmir. It's very hard to drive on this hilly terrain, especially during winter nights. My father's truck was loaded with goods which weighed about nine tons. Around midnight the road turned very steep, due to which the fully loaded truck could not proceed uphill. The road was also very narrow, so balancing the truck was becoming difficult. Though my father switched to a lower gear and hit the accelerator with as much force as possible, the truck kept slipping backwards.

My father tried using the brakes but that didn't stop the moving truck either. When all his efforts to bring the truck to a halt failed, he jumped out of the truck. My father is alive today because he jumped out. In the process, he got minor injuries on his body, but if he hadn't acted quickly when death was facing him, this could have been a major accident.

Trucking in itself is a challenge and it is made more difficult by hazardous situations like natural disasters landslides, road blockages, heavy rains, floods, etc. Then there is the danger of thefts, robberies, animal attacks especially in backward and rural areas. But risks to the drivers' lives can happen anytime, anywhere. One common threat is when the driver faces a vehicle-breakdown in a lonely area. Even a simple matter like the fusing of a headlight bulb while driving at night when visibility is normally poor can be a frightening experience. Equally frightening is when a vehicle, an animal or a human being pops out from nowhere. The risks always increase with every turn, and with every decision a truck driver makes on the road. But it's not just about risks, it is also about sustenance.

Truck drivers need to be valued for the work they do. Without them it would be impossible to transport goods, like essential commodities, objects for a comfortable life, or even luxury items, from one end of the country to another, quickly, safely and to our doorsteps.

So I pray for the safety of all truck drivers, that God grants them a long life, and brings happiness into their lives. I also pray that people get an insight into the dangerous and uncertain life of a truck driver. May they value the beauty of life, their own and of others on the road.

I love my father very much and I am very proud of him. One day I too will be able to give him a beautiful life.

13

Return of the Native

Talwar Kshitjia Sukhdev

Everyone dreams of working hard and earning enough to meet their family's needs. My father too had his own dreams. He dreamt of becoming a driver. So he took appropriate training. After completing his training he started assisting a driver in his native village. It was only after rigorous learning under his able guidance that Baba, twenty-four years old then, started working for a truck owner. From the very beginning he used to drive long distances covering states such as Kerala, Gujarat, Rajasthan and Madhya Pradesh. Later, my father got married and my sister and I were born. He is extremely proud of us and he loves us very much. He has always provided for our education and ensured that we get all the opportunities in life. He has also honed our general knowledge and taught us good behaviour. Baba never stopped my sister and me from doing anything. In fact, he always supported us. He would say, 'If you want to do anything then have a strong will and you will be successful.' Now I have completed my graduation and am taking coaching to appear for the competitive exams.

When we were young we had no idea how difficult Baba's work was. We only knew that our father drives a truck that transports goods from one place to another. Now we are older and more mature. We understand what type of work Baba has chosen. He is away from his family for eight to fifteen days at a stretch. His job demands him to travel through unknown places where he neither has any acquaintances nor does he know the place well. Even today, we feel bad when he goes away for long trips and misses out on the simple pleasures of life like spending festivals or birthdays with us.

When we were kids, Aai would drop us to school. Baba used to get ready early in the morning and before leaving for work he would ask what he should get for us. We would assume that Baba will return by night. But he would come back only after eight to fifteen days, but with everything we had asked for. We used to get very upset, because the fathers of other children would go to work in the morning and come back in the evening. When Baba would be on a trip, he'd make it a point to call us every morning before we went to school. We did not have a telephone then. Our neighbour was a policeman and he had a phone. So Baba would call there from some STD booth.

We would talk with Baba again at night. He would promise he'd come back home after we fall asleep. We would agree to have dinner and go to sleep. When we would get up in the morning we would first ask our mother, 'Aai, where is Baba, I hope he returned last night?'

Aai would feel bad but smilingly reply, 'No, my child. He could not return. But he called and asked what he should get for us. He also said that he will give a call after you get up.' During our telephonic conversations we would bombard him with questions. How was he? Did he have breakfast? When would he come back? We would request him to come back soon, to celebrate and be together on Ganapati or some other festival that would be round the corner.

This practice continues till date.

Sometimes, when he doesn't return on the expected date, we get scared. Earlier, when there were no mobiles, if we got news of a mishap in any of the areas through which Baba was supposed to be driving, we would try to gather as much information and hope and wait for him to call us.

Once, during the rainy season, Baba was driving on the Kerala-Gujarat highway. When he reached Gujarat, he unloaded the goods and was waiting to load goods from other factories. It had been raining incessantly for two days, leading to a flood situation. Baba's truck got stuck in the flood. He could not even get out of the truck to make a phone call. When we read about the floods in the newspaper, we got very worried about him. Baba had made it a practice to always keep some food items handy such as salt, chutney, lentils, rice and oil. But that stock, too, got finished quickly. As the vehicle was stuck in flood waters it was difficult to get any food. The Army and the police dropped biscuits, bread and other food items from helicopters. My father's helper tried to take the vehicle across the bridge but the river was overflowing. He was washed away and got stuck somewhere ahead.

Later when Baba narrated the incident to us, we felt terrible. We got to know that he had been stuck in that situation for eight days! We won't be able to survive like that even for a day.

We get so scared when we hear about floods, landslides and road accidents. But my father has to face these dangers every day. Some mountain roads in India are extremely dangerous and if you can't control the vehicle it can fall into the valley.

Once, my father was driving on such a mountain road and just after he crossed that stretch of road, a landslide happened right behind him. He saw it happening through the rear-view mirror. He thanked God for this narrow escape. When he tells us about such dangerous incidents it makes us feel very anxious.

In December 2004, the tsunami struck Tamil Nadu and Kerala. The whole area was badly affected. At that time, Baba was driving near the coastal area of Tamil Nadu. All the services there were shut down. We had watched the news of the tsunami and the devastation it had caused on television and read about it in the newspapers. We were desperately waiting for Baba's phone call. He also wanted to come home soon. Finally, after three days he called and told us that he was safe.

Once, our Baba had extreme back and chest pain. Aai called my mama, her brother, and they took Baba to the hospital. There it was diagnosed that he had suffered a mild heart attack. Doctors kept him in the intensive care unit for two days and discharged him only after he became completely alright. For the next one and a half months we did not send Baba to work. As Baba was at home it was difficult to meet our household expenses. But somehow we managed to run the house smoothly.

Another time, my Baba had a narrow escape in Kerala. He was driving his truck and the bus ahead of him slammed the brakes, veering the vehicle to the right to save a two-wheeler rider. Since Baba was just behind the bus, his vehicle bumped into the back of the bus. The bus turned around and hit the front side of Baba's truck. But he escaped unhurt. My sister and I can never forget these incidents.

I miss my father very much when he is away. Even if he returns home for a couple of days, for those two days our home is filled with happiness. We don't feel like celebrating any festival without him. The day Baba is at home that is the festival day for us and we celebrate. Every time he goes on a trip we ask him, 'Baba, when will you come back?'

14

The Electrical Shock

D. Tejaswini

Road safety is a most important topic and it must be highlighted in order to bring more awareness in the public, especially amongst the youth. Everyone needs to be attentive towards road traffic rules, especially children and young people who are at a significant risk of road accidents.

My father, a driver, also faced many accidents. Although he follows traffic rules, the carelessness of other drivers has been responsible for the severe injuries he has suffered. When we got news of an accident in which my father was seriously injured, my mother fainted. Our family was heartbroken and we felt very helpless at that time. He was the only breadwinner in our family.

Besides being worried about my father's accident, my mother was very anxious about our future. But by God's grace, my father recovered from the injuries. However, we had to spend a lot of money for his treatment, which we had to borrow at a high rate of interest. Then, my father struggled and worked hard day and night for many months to clear all the loans we had taken. During those days, we didn't even have proper meals.

Once when my father was driving through a forest, robbers blocked the road and stole his cell phone as well as all the money he was carrying. For some days after this, we were unable to contact Father. My younger sister and I were very worried as we couldn't talk to him for many days. After a few days, my father's employer came and told us the entire story and also promised that very soon, our father would return home safely. It was only after hearing this did we breathe a sigh of relief. That month, we had a severe shortage of money too. But my mother somehow pulled us through and kept our spirits high.

My father has faced such robberies many times. Every time this happens, my father explains everything and teaches us how to face these kinds of threats. He has also told me that as an elder child I must shoulder the responsibilities of the family after him. He makes me feel confident and encourages me to be courageous.

Recently, my father experienced an electric shock at night during the rain. His lorry was carrying a load of cement bags. It was raining heavily. In order to prevent the cement bags from getting wet, my father climbed onto the back of the truck to cover them. Suddenly, due to the heavy rain and strong winds some electric wires from a nearby electric pole, fell on my father. He got a severe electric shock, fainted and fell on the ground.

His whole body was injured. Thankfully, in a short while some people living in that area found him and rushed him to the hospital. I shudder to think of what would have happened if those people had not been there or if they hadn't admitted my father to the hospital in time.

Our family was very stressed by this incident. But again, my father got better. However, he has not fully recovered because the after-effects are still showing on his health. From this incident, I learned that though I am an engineering student, I must, and everyone else also must know how to apply at least basic first aid to provide immediate help for injured people in emergency situations like the one my father went through. It is every individual's personal responsibility to give first aid if they come across anyone who is injured, especially to road-accident victims.

15
Accident-Proof

Mali Puja Shivaji

My father is a truck driver and luckily he has never had an accident in his thirty years of driving. An accident where someone has lost his life, I mean. But minor accidents have happened. For instance, his truck once collided with an approaching vehicle. Another time a two-wheeler veered away from its track and hit the back tyre of the truck. Luckily no one was injured.

Father has never had to face a court case or imprisonment, but every driver faces natural calamities. Be it a dirt road, tar road, straight or spiral road, a driver has to always be alert and have his eyes on the road while driving.

There is one memorable incident in my baba's life. This happened when Baba was working as a senior driver for a goods carrier. The year was 1998, and his salary was ₹1000 per month He had been assigned to carry 350 bags of green chilies from Dondaicha to Nagpur.

After the job had been completed and all the bags successfully unloaded, Baba started driving back home. It was late in the evening, the sky was dark but there was bright moonlight. Baba's companion, a young boy, was sleeping by his side on the passenger seat since he was very tired. At some point during the night, however, the boy woke up and requested Baba to give him a chance to drive the truck. Baba smiled, obliged and advised him, 'Be careful, and use the second gear instead of the third. Also keep one foot on the brake.'

In the beginning, Baba sat beside him and taught him what to do. As it was dark and the truck was moving slowly, all the trucks had gone ahead, leaving their truck behind. After a while, they spotted a group of more than ten men under a tree on the side of the road. Before they could realise what was happening, there was a sound of glass shattering. Some object, probably a stone, had smashed the windshield of the truck. The young boy was badly injured.

That object was thrown at the person on the driver's seat. For a moment, Baba was unable to understand what was happening. Glass pieces had pierced his cheeks, neck and also his eyes. The boy had taken his hands off the steering wheel and was crying in extreme pain. Despite such a scary situation, Baba did not waste a single moment. He somehow managed to move the boy aside, climbed into the driver's seat, put the vehicle in third gear, slammed his foot on the accelerator and kept the truck moving.

He did not stop the truck until they reached a village where he took the boy to a hospital. However, after seeing his condition, the doctor started questioning Baba about how these injuries had happened to the boy. The doctor insisted that he would be able to admit the boy in the hospital only if a police complaint was filed first.

My Baba was forced to take the vehicle to the next village where he lied to the doctor that the boy was driving a truck on a deserted road, had dozed off and crashed his vehicle. At that time a stone on the road had hurt his chest. But as the doctor did not have enough facilities to treat the boy, he just gave a tetanus injection and dressed his wounds. After they reached Dondaicha, my father narrated the whole incident to the manager. But the manager barely paid for the boy's treatment. Whatever little he did give was given unwillingly.

When my father described the condition of that young boy to us, I literally got goose bumps. Everyone in my family was shocked to hear about this experience. Baba said that the cabinet of the truck was stained with blood and there was a blood-stained stone in a corner. It must have weighed at least half a kilo. After listening to this incident, I realised the apathy of the public, of those in the medical services and of the employers. Before I end I would like to make one small request. If ever such an accident occurs, for the sake of humanity, first give treatment to the driver and if he is found guilty of any wrongdoing, punish him later.

16

Death of a Friend

Sharmeen Parveen

Those days robberies were very common in Assam. So when my father had to go to Assam with the truck, we got worried. We did not have mobile phones then. Our neighbour had a telephone, so we used to talk with Papa on their phone. One day, through their phone, we got the news that Papa had been admitted to a hospital. The hospital had called that number because Papa had given it as his contact number. We were very frightened. It was not easy to travel so far, but still some of our relatives rushed to Assam.

Till they reached Assam no one knew what had happened to Papa and why he was in the hospital. Only when our relatives met the people who had taken Papa first to the police station and then to the hospital, did they learn the truth.

We were told that it was raining heavily that night. The roads had become very slippery. As there are more chances of an accident on a slippery road, Papa had parked the truck on the side.

Papa, the other driver and the conductor, went to sleep. Suddenly ten-twelve people came and started trying to open the window of the truck. All of them had weapons. Papa and the conductor were unaware of what was happening as they were fast asleep. The other driver tried to stop the attackers but he was not able to do so. Hearing all the commotion Papa and the conductor woke up. Before Papa and the conductor could realise what was happening one of the robbers fired at the other driver.

Both Papa and the conductor succeeded in getting out of the other window and running away. The conductor ran into the jungle and hid there. But Papa kept running on the road as the robbers were following him. Suddenly Papa saw a bus passing by. Papa got into the moving bus. That bus was returning from a marriage function. The way Papa ran and climbed the bus, people inside the bus thought he was a thief as that area was notorious for robberies.

The people in the bus beat Papa and injured him badly. Somehow Papa told them what had happened with him and requested them to take him to the nearest police station. They agreed and Papa informed the police about the incident. The police reached the spot but by then the other driver had died. Papa was already severely injured and the news of the death of the other driver affected him so much that he fell unconscious. Then the same people in the bus took him to the hospital. Our relatives brought Papa and the dead body of the other driver back home. Papa had fractured his leg and hand, and he had injuries on several other parts of his body. He was not able to walk.

The death of Papa's fellow driver and the severe injuries that he himself had sustained affected us all. The death of that driver was especially distressful for his as well as our family. But by the grace of God my papa and the conductor's lives were saved. Since then, Papa has never gone there with the truck.

Papa has had a very difficult life. He has had to struggle a lot. But he never shies away from hard work. He has faced all the difficulties of life with his honesty and dedication. I have witnessed all the adverse incidents that happened to him since my childhood, when the financial condition of our family was weak. Now everything is alright. Now I want to complete my education and support my father so that he won't be alone during any difficult period.

17

Happy Family

Meenakshi Saini

My father is a truck driver and we have learned a lot from his experiences. Left to himself, he would never drive at night for it is not safe at all. Somehow, robbers always know if drivers are travelling alone. They lie in wait and the moment a truck crosses a speed breaker, they cut the ropes and steal the goods.

My father has told me that in several states, especially UP, Bihar and Assam, when drivers go to file a police report, the police blame the drivers instead, for selling the goods in the open market. Even if they do agree to file a report, they demand ₹10,000. Very often my father has no choice but to stay hungry even while working. If there is a traffic jam due to an accident or the road is blocked for some other reason, my father cannot leave his vehicle. So he is forced to go without food and water on those days.

Sometimes while travelling at night, the police trouble him and demand money as bribes. My father has also told me how it is not easy to drive at night. The bright lights of the vehicles coming from the opposite side make it very difficult to see the road. Worse, if a truck breaks down en route, it is almost impossible to park the vehicle on the side of the road as there is the danger of colliding with other vehicles.

After listening to my father's stories, sometimes I wish that the government makes more efforts to establish proper rules and laws for assisting truck drivers so that they don't face such problems.

Once, it was late in the evening, when my father left for Guwahati after loading coal in his truck. He had just about covered a distance of thirty kilometres when a red car driving on the same side as my father's truck asked him to stop. There was a driver and two persons inside the car. My father refused to stop. Since six other trucks were accompanying him, the car driver tried to stop the others instead. However, no other truck driver stopped his vehicle. After some time all seven vehicles, including that car, stopped at a tea shop.

At this point the owner of the red car asked the others about the truck driver they were trying to initially stop, which was my father. When they asked why he wanted to know, the red car owner said that he also belonged to Haryana and wanted to meet him. My father was not convinced. He was still talking to the car driver, trying to figure out the real reason why he was chasing him, when the man drew out his revolver. At this point, all fifteen truck drivers travelling with my father snatched the man's revolver and reported him to the nearby police station. It was later found that the car driver had intended to stop the truck and rob it. The police started an enquiry into the case and my father and his friends were asked to leave the place. Thankfully, on this particular occasion, my father as well as his other friends came back home unhurt.

Another incident I'd like to share took place in 1998. The government of Gujarat had ordered a hundred cycles for school children. These had to be transported from Haryana. My father loaded his truck at Sonepat Atlas Factory, reached the location, handed over the goods to the company's client and stayed at his place. Early the next morning, he started driving his truck. It had been raining very hard and he could barely see beyond a few metres. While trying to negotiate a turn, he noticed another truck trying to overtake a tractor-trailer. My father realised that his truck was about to collide with the truck ahead. To save the truck, he stopped. But in the process, his vehicle overturned. The way his truck fell, there was no danger of it coming in the way of any other vehicle. Thankfully, on this occasion too he was saved.

There was one time when my father was on his way to Sonepat from Guwahati. His truck was loaded with coal and he and the conductor were travelling by themselves with no other accompanying vehicle. That's probably the reason why a car started following him. They stopped a little ahead of him and my father's truck was therefore forced to stop too. There were five persons in the car. They got into my father's truck and pulled out the keys. They caught my father and the conductor, and gagged them. They dragged them to a cane field, tied their hands and legs and left them there. It was early morning by the time some women found them. They untied them. Immediately, my father went to check on the truck. It was still there, but his money, about ₹4800 had been stolen. My father left for Garhmukteshwar from there and filed a police report. The police started searching for the robbers and allowed him to leave. My father reached home tired, bruised and in need of rest, to recover from the incident.

When my father tells us about these experiences we end up in tears. We feel very bad for him and constantly worry about him. Many times, he isn't able to spend festivals with us. This year he was not with us for Raksha Bandhan and we missed him a lot. But I am proud of my father and thankful to him for grooming me and my three siblings in such a way that we always want to get ahead in life. No matter what happens to him, my father ensures our happiness. Ours is one happy family and it's all because of him.

18

Punished Unfairly

Chitralaxmi Swain

My father has been driving a truck for the last twenty-five years and it is his driving that has provided for the education of all my brothers and sisters and also the wedding of my eldest sister.

My father has always advised me and my siblings to never be selfish. 'You must not do anything which hurts others,' is what he has taught us.

With such high ideals you can imagine how my father leads his life, dealing with all his responsibilities in the best way possible. And yet, sometimes life tests you, punishes you for no fault of yours.

On 16 November 2016, my father was going from Rourkela (Orissa) to Vishakhapatnam with a load of some heavy goods in his vehicle. Due to the bad condition of the road, he had to pass through a village where his vehicle collided with an electric pole and the pole broke. As a result, the power supply to the village was cut off. Immediately, all the people of the village stopped my father and surrounded the vehicle. Many started abusing him.

My father kept apologising but they were so furious, they were not ready to listen to him. Thankfully, the sarpanch of the village arrived at the spot. My father told him everything and requested him to provide a solution to his problem. The sarpanch decided that my father should leave the vehicle in the village till a new pole gets erected and that he would have to bear all the expenses. My father agreed to the terms of the sarpanch and gave ₹15,000 to him. He had to live there for three days after that.

After three days when the power supply had been restored and my father was about to leave, another problem surfaced. My father saw all the villagers coming towards him and became nervous to see the sarpanch leading the crowd. The sarpanch told my father to pay for all the damage to their goods such as televisions, fans, coolers, refrigerators, etc., due to the broken pole and said, 'Till you pay the total amount, you will not be allowed to go out of the village with the vehicle.'

My father pleaded with them. He was only a driver, how could he give so much money to them? 'My salary is ₹5000 and above all, my master will not be able to give me this much money,' my father tried to make the sarpanch understand. He also informed all the villagers that he was forced to pass through the village because of the bad condition of the road. And if the goods he was carrying did not reach the destination on time, the truck owner would abuse him, but the people of the village remained unmoved.

Then my father called the owner and told him everything. 'I tried my best to solve the problem amicably but failed. Now you will have to come here,' he said. After hearing all this, the owner talked to the sarpanch and asked him about the money. The sarpanch demanded ₹65,000. The next day, the owner's son brought the money and gave it to the sarpanch. My father was allowed to leave for Vishakhapatnam. The accident that happened in the village that day had its effect on our whole family. My father's master deducted ₹80,000 from his salary, which would have covered us for fourteen months.

In all the accidents that occur in India, almost ninety percent of the time people hold drivers guilty. This is wrong. A driver is also a human being and deserves sympathy. But hardly anyone cares.

19

Friends and Enemies

J. Maria Asuritha Riya

My father has been driving his own lorry for the past thirty years. During these years, not only my father, but even we, his family, have come across many incidents that are unforgettable.

In his professional life my father has gone through many difficulties. He has faced dacoits and robbers. He has had to drive through natural calamities and extreme weather conditions. But even then he has never quit. He is that passionate about his job.

While my father may have come across many undesirable people, he has also been given the opportunity to meet good human beings.

In a world full of selfish people, my father is different. He believes in equality, and respects every one's rights. In order to bring control and prevent wrong practices in the transport business, he established a Lorry Owners' Welfare Society and to this date it is running successfully. He has confronted some challenges in the running of this society and many people are jealous of his progress, yet he keeps working to improve the conditions of lorry owners, his major aim being to stop the practice of overloading of trucks.

However, that is not to say that he doesn't have any problems. In fact, he has a lot of enemies. We are always scared for his life and spend sleepless nights whenever he goes out during the night to respond to a call.

Once, at about 1 o'clock in the night, my father heard someone talking in whispers near our lorry. When he went to check, he saw some people trying to open the diesel tank. The moment they saw my father, they fled in a car. My father was unarmed at the time. All he had was his cell phone. Since there was not enough light he could not even note down the number of the car. My father then called two of his friends, George and Annachi. George had my father's two-wheeler with him. My father explained what had happened and together, all three of them went in search of the thieves.

When they were about two kilometres away from the scene of the incident, they saw a group of people threatening a lorry driver at knifepoint and trying to steal diesel from his lorry. Once again, the moment the troublemakers saw the headlights of the two-wheeler, all three of them tried to flee in their car. My father drove his two-wheeler as fast as the car, but unfortunately, he fell down and was dragged by the car for some distance. George managed to break the glass of the window next to the driver's seat and forced the driver to stop the car.

When he caught hold of the driver's neck, the driver attacked him with an iron rod and hit George on his head. George fell on the road and started bleeding profusely. Seeing him in such a state, my father was in a fix. He called two more of his friends for help and sent George to the hospital along with them in a car. He then went on to report the incident to the Kallakudi Police Station.

My father returned home at 5 a.m. and knocked on the door. He was soaked in blood, and we thought he was injured. But he assured us nothing had happened to him and that he was safe. He changed his clothes, took some money and left without informing us where he was going. My mom couldn't stop weeping and her condition worried us. We felt relieved only when my father returned home and told us the entire story. He informed us that the thieves had been caught. We were very worried after this incident and are always so whenever he goes out for his work at night.

For the last one year now, he has been the president of the Lorry Owners' Welfare Association. And he is still fighting against cement factory owners for overloading goods vehicles. Due to this he is facing a lot of problems. When you try to do something good, you tend to earn a lot of enemies. I am glad my father is brave and a match for all who stand against him.

20

Thwarting Armed Robbers

Suneeta Singh

My father has been a truck driver for the last twenty-five years.

This incident happened in Gwalior, Madhya Pradesh, in 2014. My father was driving the truck, and there was a helper accompanying him. The area he was driving through was known to be unsafe. At around 4 a.m., three people suddenly appeared as if from nowhere, stood in the middle of the road and forced the truck to stop. The three armed robbers attacked my father. They snatched his mobile phone and wallet.

The helper was clever. He didn't have the courage to face them so he ran away to save his own life leaving Papa alone. Papa had a faint hope that they would allow him to go, but the main aim of the robbers was to hijack the truck. They made Papa get down from the truck and asked him for the keys. Papa refused to hand it to them. They held a gun to Papa's head. Like any other person facing that kind of dangerous situation, he also thought his life was over.

As I am writing this story, sitting beside Papa, he tells me why he considers that day as the luckiest of his life. He was saved by sheer luck! Being a very strong man, he did not lose his cool. He put the robbers in a decision-dilemma by saying that he had more money in the truck, which he could share with them if he was released. The impressed robbers allowed him to go inside the truck to get the money. Papa took the chance! He grabbed an iron rod, which he had kept hidden behind his seat and attacked two of the robbers with all his strength.

None of them expected their prey to counter-attack so violently. Two of them were badly injured from the sudden attack while the third one, distracted, rushed towards his accomplices to attend to them. Papa found that it was the best time to flee and quickly went back to the truck. Sitting in the cabin he locked it from inside, started the engine without delay and sped away. He drove continuously for three hours before stopping at a petrol pump. He was happy that he had escaped alive!

It was a joyous day for our family too. For quite some time my mom had been trying to call Papa. His phone was switched off. We were also waiting for his call as we needed to arrange money for our school fees. My mother, my younger brother and I had been praying to God to send him back home as soon as possible.

We could not control our tears when we received a call from an unknown number and heard Papa's voice at a time when all of us were eagerly waiting for his call. I got goose bumps on my arms and tears in my eyes when I heard about this incident. At the end of the call we were extremely happy to know that he was fine and would return home soon. We got our smiles back on our faces.

I salute my father for being a brave driver. I am fortunate that I could write something on my father and I'm thankful to Mahindra Saarthi Abhiyaan for this platform.

21

Risks

Pooja Dahiya

My father is a highly experienced driver. He often goes on long trips and though we would like him to be home by dinner time, that is seldom possible. He is usually away from home for three to four months at a stretch. He has to drive through difficult terrains in mountainous areas, and on sharp zigzag roads; so all of us wait for him anxiously. Whenever he is late, many scary thoughts run through our minds, our biggest worry being his safety. We keep looking at the door, wishing and praying he returns home safely.

Having observed my father so closely, I know that a driver's life is full of risks. If the weather turns inclement, for instance, and it starts raining heavily, then landslides can occur and these can block the movement of vehicles. When there is a thunderstorm there is no telephone connectivity. The entire family is in the grip of fear since the head of the family is out driving and there is no contact with him. It is only when my father comes back home that we all breathe a sigh of relief. In fact, when my father arrives, the mood in our house suddenly turns festive. Every member of the family wants to spend as much time with him as possible. Each one of us is curious to hear about his adventures to distant places. He is the centre of attention for everybody when he is at home.

One day my father was driving his truck when someone on the way asked him for a lift. Since the man looked helpless, my father allowed him to get into the truck. As they went along my father noticed that some people were trying to surround the vehicle and block its path. That was when my father became suspicious. My father did not intend to halt the truck but the man sitting beside him suddenly slapped him and forced him to stop immediately.

But my father gathered the courage to push the man out of the vehicle and drive off until he reached the nearest police station. Once he got there he narrated the entire incident to the police who carried out a search of the truck and found a bag full of cartridges in it. They took my father into custody. My father explained to them that the bag belonged to the man who he had given a lift to. But the police did not believe him and tortured him.

Many days later when the police busted the gang of robbers to which that man belonged, my father easily identified him. The man made a complete confession under intense police interrogation. The police ensured the delivery of goods in my father's truck and also apologised to him and released him.

A driver has to face several difficulties during his journey such as dacoity, traffic jams, natural disasters, etc. To avoid such incidents, there should be proper lighting on the highways. There should be a public helpline or telephone and telecommunication centres that drivers can use to contact their families in case they are stranded on the road. There should be ample patrolling of streets by traffic police, and traffic signals installed at important junctions to deal with traffic jams. There should be drainage along the road to sluice out the water that gets accumulated in low-lying areas. Moreover, tar coal should be used in the building of roads to strengthen them. Special attention should be paid to the quality of material used in road construction so that drivers do not have to face any problems while driving. This will not only ensure minimum risks to the drivers' lives but also help in the safe delivery of goods.

22

Travel Travails

Yasmeen

My father has been driving for about thirty-seven years. During this time he has driven a bus, a tempo, a tractor and other vehicles too. After driving all these vehicles, he took to driving a truck which, compared to the rest, is a large vehicle. He is now recognised as a skilled truck driver. A truck driver's life is full of challenges. He has to face all kinds of adversities. I wish to share some of them with you. I heard about this incident from my father during my childhood.

My father has been to Madhya Pradesh, Maharashtra, Goa, Tamil Nadu, Rajasthan, Gujarat, Delhi, Chattisgarh, Jharkhand, Orissa, Bihar, Bengal, Assam, Meghalaya, Nagaland, Arunachal Pradesh, Mizoram and Tripura. Apart from these he has been to Nepal, Bhutan and Bangladesh, which are foreign territories.

One day, Father had loaded his vehicle and was going from Indore to Kanpur. Around midnight, at a place called

Makshi, one of the truck tyres got punctured. When he got down to change the tyre, eight-ten goons surrounded him and held a knife to his throat. They stole about ₹20,000, which he had received for carrying the goods and for diesel. Apart from this the amount he had kept for his daily expenses was also taken away.

Not only did they take his money, the goons beat him badly till he was bleeding. After that they led him to a field about a hundred metres away and started chirping like sparrows so that the villagers wouldn't suspect anything. They tied up my father's hands and legs and took away his warm clothes as well since it was a cold night.

There was no one nearby. My father was desperate. Because his limbs were tied, he was helpless. He spent the winter night shivering. The villagers, who went there at dawn, found him. They untied him and helped him with whatever he needed since he was in a terrible state.

Another incident took place in 1986. My father was travelling from Assam to Kanpur. At Kishanganj he had to face a road blockade. The main road was completely damaged due to the floods. The Calcutta-Patna road via Kanpur was entirely blocked, and he was stuck in the floods for forty days. He had to face many troubles, most of which can't be expressed in words. Initially, food was organised somehow, but soon the shops nearby ran out of rations. Though the Army jawans used to bring relief materials, the villagers treated it as if it was only for them and did not share it with any of the travellers.

At that time our financial condition was not good. My family did not know where Father was and what state he was in. My mother and grandmother were always anxious, thinking of the possible dangers. My mother became ill due to the stress she went through. But there was no money for treatment.

In 1992, my father was driving from Kanpur to Bombay. While passing through Madhya Pradesh, a tractor hit Father's truck from the rear. The tractor driver lost four fingers. The police reached the site immediately. It was an accident for which the tractor driver was to blame. Yet, my father was accused and the police filed a case against him. The police harassed him for no fault of his.

Whenever my father goes out of the country to load the vehicle in Nepal, Bhutan, or Bangladesh, he takes a long time to return. He is the sole breadwinner and all the family members are entirely dependent on his earnings. When he doesn't come home on time we get worried. Mother and I have to take over all his duties during his absence. Whenever he is delayed due to a vehicle-breakdown or traffic jams, we have to face financial difficulties. At times we are unable to pay the school fees on time. We don't have money for clothes and eatables on festivals. Sometimes we have to make do with eating dry bread.

When I was a child, I used to ask my mother to tell Father to come home soon. When I grew up and heard about his struggles while travelling, I felt deeply about the way he has faced problems without any complaints. He does all that to give us a good life. I must learn that I too must be ready to face the struggles of life like my father. I will complete my education, and be self-sufficient. I will not be dependent on Father for my needs, for he has spent more than half his life facing challenges and obstacles. He could not eat home food and have meals on time, he often could not get the pleasure of being with the family in a home. Be it the freezing cold winter or the blazing hot summer, he kept driving. He has driven through jungles and mountains, and areas he was unfamiliar with. Despite not being able to understand the languages of the places he has driven through and coming across unfriendly people, he continues to drive for his livelihood.

I am proud of my father. Today he has the reputation of being a good, safe and reliable truck driver. He has trained many other drivers too. Currently, he is driving well to earn a living.

23

Driving The Nation

Vatika Kumar

My father is a truck driver. He drives his loaded truck day and night to ensure that the goods reach their destination safely and on time. His job has no fixed timings. He leaves home and then is gone for days, even weeks. When he doesn't come back home in time, all of us worry a lot. My mother feels relaxed and happy only when he is back home, safe and sound.

We are a family of five—my father, mother, brother, sister and me. I'm the eldest among my siblings. My father, the only earning member of the family, works very hard to ensure all of us get a good education. My brother and sister are studying in a private school. My mother is a housewife.

There is a common misconception about truck drivers, that they are drug addicts, alcoholics and habitual offenders. This isn't true at all. Truck drivers have families and they work very hard to keep their family comfortable and provided for.

Driving a truck isn't easy and accidents can happen anytime. My father has had more than his share of bad luck.

On 10 February 2004, he was attacked and looted by a gang of robbers. It was around 10.30 p.m. He was returning to Mumbai via Delhi and while he was driving near Dhaula Kuan, suddenly a van stopped him. A few men jumped out of it and overpowered my father. They thrust a knife to his neck and pointed a pistol at him. They took the ₹10,000 he was carrying, threw him in a nearby forest and drove away with the truck. They had beaten him so badly that he was unconscious. Till date there are scars on his body. One of the men wanted to kill him but thank God the others stopped him. After some time, my father regained consciousness, and managed to go to a nearby dhaba to get help. He then went to the police station to lodge an FIR.

Father was in a state of shock when he came home, and had to be hospitalised. He was so ill that he stayed at home for a month. I will never forget the moment he walked in, bleeding, injured and in a lot of pain.

The police recovered the looted truck within a week but they couldn't get the goods it was carrying. The men who attacked him had sold off everything. The insurance company paid for all the looted items but that took almost two years. This incident shocked everyone at home, especially my father. He could have been killed by those men.

This was not the only time my father was attacked on the road. A similar incident took place, but this time in Rajasthan. These kinds of dangers are faced by all truck drivers. They are easy targets for looters.

Another awful incident happened when his truck caught fire because of an electrical fault. Happenings like these don't just get us worried and scared, they are also the reason why our lives can never get better. They shatter our dreams and hopes.

Truck driving is a tough job. There's a saying among truck drivers, 'Be aware or face an accident.'

Truck transport is an important part of the country's economy. The police and administration should take care of the transportation sector and protect the truck drivers from getting looted, injured and killed. There must be strict rules and regulations to ensure safety at night for smooth working and driving.

If truck transportation stops, it will result in a huge loss for the economy; so it's essential that the administration pays special attention to this sector and the truck drivers.

I appeal to the Government of India to enforce stringent rules and regulations for the safety of truck drivers. Truck drivers should be able to do their job at night and during the day without any fear.

24

The Unusual Journeys of My Father

Prableen Kaur

I remember that it was summer and we were living a normal, happy life when suddenly the phone rang. We were worried as it was an unusual time for the phone to ring at that hour. We could at once feel that it was a call regarding some unfortunate news about my father, who was driving continuously in a mountainous terrain. We were right!

My father was in a terrible condition—he had been trapped in a landslide far away, but we couldn't do anything as it was very late in the night. All we could do is pray to God for his safety. Early in the morning, when we were assured by the nearest police station that my father was rescued, it seemed that God had answered all our prayers. That was the happiest moment for us as my father had survived a huge misfortune.

We reside in the state of Jammu and Kashmir where the hilly roads become slippery and dangerous during the rainy season. Driving on such roads is extremely unsafe. The unfavourable weather and the conditions faced by my father as a truck driver are incomparable. He has to drive through areas like the 'Khooni Nallah', a spot known for accidents because of shooting stones and deep gorges. But still, he fights adverse conditions each day just to feed us.

There are innumerable stories about the tough conditions and horrifying moments experienced by my father, incidents that shook him many times.

When my father was trapped in the landslide, there was no connectivity on his phone. We tried to contact him throughout the night but he was not reachable. The news channels kept telecasting updates and pictures of the mishap but we were helpless. We tried our level best to connect with him but it was all in vain. We had started losing hope, but it was the strength of our beloved mother who motivated us and kept us positive. Fortunately, the next evening, Father called us and we were overjoyed to just hear his voice. We prayed that nothing should ever harm him.

Once, while driving to Delhi, he faced yet another dreadful situation which makes me wonder how someone can think of getting money at the cost of destroying another person's family. It is inhuman. My father was attacked by robbers who threw eggs at the windshield. Despite not being able to see ahead clearly and having no idea of what was happening, he didn't apply the brakes and kept moving. My father believes that when you are on the highway and if something strange happens in the middle of the night, you should understand that things will become worse soon. If he would have used the wipers, the egg yolk would have spread across the windscreen and he wouldn't have been able to see anything at all. Then the scenario would have been different. But he understood the situation and dealt with it smartly and bravely. Neither did he use the wipers nor did he halt the truck, and thus, he was saved. He is our hero. I am really proud of him.

Another time my father was driving to Leh-Ladakh, in the greater Himalayas, to unload his truck, when he met with one more challenging situation. On an extremely cold night, he found himself stuck because there had been heavy snowfall and the roads had been blocked for ten days. The amount of oxygen in the air decreases to a great extent upon crossing Totila Pass. Only the Almighty could have helped him during that time. My father had limited ration to survive on. It was a difficult task for the PWD department to clear the roads and they could not do so until the evening. My father was left with only two options—either to starve to death or take a risk. He decided to take that risk. When he later described the steep valleys where he could see no road because everything was covered with snow, my blood went cold and I shivered with fear.

Anyway, he decided to drive. The road was slippery and single lane. Shooting stones made it extremely difficult for him to continue his journey. Yet, he kept moving. The sound of the shooting stones falling on top of his truck was frightening. He was praying all the while. Unfortunately, one of the tyres got punctured on that slippery road. But he didn't accept defeat and kept moving the entire night until early morning when he crossed that terrifying area and was out of danger.

Whenever our breadwinner, our hero, is not back in time we wonder if he is safe or in some kind of trouble due to the dangerous life he leads. We always pray that he is away from any kind of danger. Whenever we see him, we become hopeful that one day we will achieve success because of the pains he takes and the hard work he puts in for us to get a better life. He is our real hero, who fights against all odds just to fill our stomachs and to shape our future. His dedication towards his work motivates us as he never tries to escape from his responsibilities. There are countless hurdles in the way of truckers but they are bold enough to face any challenge and earn for their families.

One thing I have learned from my father's experience is that hard work is the key to success, in any field of work.

25
A Scary Journey

Aksha Khan

Once, my father was taking Kaagda Ji Mandli passengers from Mathura to Himachal for a Ramleela performance. The Mahindra bus was twenty-six metres in length and it could accommodate twenty-seven people. One person, who was supposed to play the role of Ravan, was also present in the bus. While travelling from Haryana to Punjab, in order to avoid toll tax payment, my father chose the route that leads through hilly areas.

However, even after driving for hours, my father realised that he was nowhere near the destination. Around 10 p.m., there was a dust storm. Due to the storm, the bus started tilting towards a pit but fortunately, my father is an experienced driver. He told everybody to open the windows of the bus. They followed his instructions and soon, the bus became stable. The terrain was such that there was the danger of being attacked by wild animals too. The roads were damaged and the bus could not even cover fifty kilometres that night. My father missed the way to the main road and no one was available to direct them towards the right road. Every passenger was worried and started chanting 'Radhe-Radhe Gobind-Gobind', praying for safety.

Around 3 a.m. they heard strange sounds from inside the bus. My father and conductor got down from the bus and found that a tyre had punctured. They changed the tyre in the light of a candle. After travelling for a while they noticed a village, but not a villager could be seen. Later they found two villagers and asked them the directions to the highway. After they showed them the path, my father and his passengers were finally back on track.

Sometime later, my father stopped the bus next to a restaurant where everybody had snacks and finally went on to reach Kaagda safely. He stayed there for ten days, and when he came home, we felt relieved. His arrival was akin to celebrating Eid! He had got us gifts and we all sat next to him. After having dinner, he told us about the incident. My mother started crying. She told him, 'You should always take care of the passengers who have complete faith in you.'

26

Unpredictable Trips

Mounika Poojari

My father is a trucker. A long-distance trucker's life is full of adventure. He goes through many bizarre incidents on the road. I have grown up in a working-class family hearing stories of my father's life-threatening experiences every day.

Once, my father was driving on the highway towards Bhubaneswar. It was afternoon. Suddenly he saw something from a distance. It seemed like dry leaves blowing in the wind towards the road. The sight puzzled him. It was a rocky area without any big trees around. Moreover, he had never seen leaves blowing in waves like that before. He rolled up the glass windows and continued driving. As he drew closer, he realised that the 'leaves' were actually migrating honeybees. They were crossing the highway in thousands.

Initially, he thought slowing down might be better. But the aggressive honeybees probably felt annoyed by the presence of the truck in their path. They attacked the vehicle from all sides. My father had to speed away. He stopped at the next truck stop and called his co-driver who was sleeping in the bunk bed behind him, to help him fill the fuel tank. He told him the story of his unusual experience. The co-driver did not believe him in the beginning. But the moment they stepped out of the truck, they found hundreds of honeybees stuck all over the truck—some of their caked bodies were on the tyres, some were crushed under the wheels and many more were half-dead, trapped under the cover of the loaded truck. It was so sad.

My father has escaped a violent storm too. He was driving through a deserted area when strong winds started blowing across the road. However, he decided to carry on till he reached a village. By that time the wind had become fiercer. He was about to pull over and take shelter in the dhaba nearby, when all of a sudden he noticed another truck with a trailer parked on the roadside being tossed like a toy, barely a hundred yards away!

He later told me that he wanted to call home at that moment; he thought he was going to die. He somehow took the truck to the roadside pull-off, opened both doors and windows of the vehicle and crawled towards the dhaba. The small thatched front space was overcrowded as all truckers and helpers had taken shelter there. The powerful wind was shaking the walls violently. The hospitable dhaba owner then invited all of them into his home behind the dhaba.

The storm stopped after a couple of hours. All those who had taken shelter inside came out to discover that the dhaba had been completely destroyed. Several trucks were lying on their sides, tossed by the wind. Only those vehicles that had their doors and windows open, were saved.

The stories my father tells me have made me aware of road safety issues, and how safe driving practices help a long-distance truck driver survive unpredictable and dangerous situations. My father emphasises the value of education. He tells me that education is everything. That it helps in achieving whatever a person wants in life. He also says that every time we open our doors, we find new experiences. We must continue to make new commitments to keep growing in every way. It is our duty to discover how we can positively influence the world around us.

Our life brings different kinds of experiences—some strange, some memorable and some dangerous. All of them teach us some lesson or the other. Our duty is to apply the learning in a positive way.

27

Life Saver

Waghamare Puja Dagadu

We are a family of three: my father, mother and I. My mother goes out to do household chores and my father is a driver. He has studied up till class five. He goes out for work every morning at 4 o'clock, without having a morsel of food or a drop of water. Usually, it is very dark when he leaves. And that is why we feel very anxious about him. How will he go? How will the roads be? How will he drive if it is raining? We worry more because he drives alone—no one accompanies him. Life is not easy for us.

The other day, there was an election and my father had gone to a village with twenty to thirty men and women voters in the truck with him. By the time they started their return journey, it was very late in the night. They had to drive through a jungle and there were no other vehicles on the dark road. Moreover, they had to take a different route while returning, not the one they had taken earlier. It was a more dangerous road.

When they were almost half way through, ten to fifteen goondas suddenly came out of nowhere and surrounded the vehicle. They had big weapons, knives, daggers, etc. They made my father stop, pointed their guns at the vehicle and started demanding money. My father had to literally fall at the feet of those goons. 'We are poor men. I beg of you. Please let us go,' he pleaded. But they did not relent and pointed the gun at my father's head. My father started sweating profusely. He had also started trembling. He thought it was the end of his life.

He begged the goondas again and again to let them go. 'I have a wife and a little girl. Who will look after them? They would be left all alone without me. Let me go,' he said to them. Right then the head of the gang came and told the others to let my father go. Even then, my father had to pay two thousand rupees to them.

All this while, the people in the vehicle kept sitting silently. However, just as the goons left, all of them stood up and appreciated his courage. 'All of us were hiding beneath the seats and you dealt with them all alone. What to say, you are like God to us,' they told him.

The next day when my father returned home and told us what had happened, we got very frightened. My mother and I hugged each other and started weeping. But we felt glad that nothing had happened to my father. Many, many thanks to God that my father returned home safely. What happened to my father should not happen to anyone else and we must work to ensure road safety in our country. That is the reason why I have decided to work for road safety in our country once I complete my MA.

28

The Bail

Bhavna Gautam

We are three sisters and one brother, and along with my mother, we completely depend on my father's income for survival. He is a truck driver and has been driving for the last fifteen years. He started his career by driving a rented auto. He had to work as per the instructions of his boss, and had to immediately go for duty whenever his master called him, even when he would be midway through his meal.

Whenever there were any kind of losses, whether it was his fault or not, the owner would deduct the amount from my father's salary. After doing this for three to four years my father became a truck driver. He worked hard to become a truck driver because working as an auto driver for somebody else was very difficult. He earned nothing more than ₹3000 per month. It was difficult to provide for four children and bear the expenses of a household on such a meagre salary. Our grandfather and grandmother also live with us.

Once, my mother fell ill and my father was travelling on work. We did not have the money for our mother's treatment. Our grandfather got my mother treated after taking a loan from someone.

Four years ago, my father had gone on a long trip when his truck broke down at night. My uncle was with him. He was forced to park the truck by the roadside and sleep there. Sometime during the night when my father and uncle were fast asleep, a thief came and stole the battery. My father and uncle came to know about the theft only in the morning. When the owner of the truck was told about it, he got very angry and held the driver, that is my father, responsible for the incident and deducted ₹15,000 from his salary, due to which our entire family suffered.

That aside, we had to listen to a lot of insults and rude words from our school teachers as our financial condition was very bad and we ended up being late at paying our school fees. Sometimes our father had to take a loan for it. Our father had to hear a lot of criticism from many people.

Once, he was returning from Kanpur when his truck broke down on an isolated stretch of road in Rusalabad. There was no mechanic to be found so my father and uncle were forced to stop there. Just as they lay down, eight thieves attacked, and beat them with lathis. In the morning, the people passing by noticed my father and uncle lying unconscious and got them admitted to a hospital.

There was a fracture in my father's leg and his head and hands were also badly hurt. It took some months for him to recover from that. But two months later, a small lump surfaced on my father's leg. It kept getting bigger with time. When he consulted a doctor, he was advised to get it operated upon, otherwise the lump could turn cancerous. After the surgery my father could not go to work for some time. The condition of our finances deteriorated further. The owner of the truck did not pay my father's salary for that month and also withheld the salary of other months and demanded ₹10,000 from us for the damage to the truck.

My father borrowed ₹20,000 from one of his friends, gave the owner ₹10,000 and the remaining ₹10,000 was spent on the surgery. That month was very difficult for our family. There was no ration at home. During the day, we used to go to our uncle's house where our aunty would give us five rotis for the whole family and we would spend the day eating those rotis only. At night, we would sleep after drinking water. We were turned out of school due to non-payment of fees. Other schools did not admit us. Finally, we got admission in another school after the payments were made.

Our father did not rest properly even after the surgery and went back to driving his truck the very next month. Despite his poor health, he works very hard. When he goes out, we always worry for him, wondering if he is okay, whether he has taken his food or not, and whether he has taken his medicines on time. Sometimes our father comes home very late and has to go back again the next morning, without taking enough rest.

A few days back, he was driving his truck when suddenly the glass of the windshield in front exploded and fell on his left hand due to which a vein on his hand got cut. A bus was coming from the opposite direction but my father had closed his eyes due to the pain. We still do not know how he managed to save the truck. He says that if someone saved him, it was God. Later, as a lot of blood had been lost, he fainted. An uncle who had accompanied my father took him to the hospital. When my father regained consciousness, there were eight stitches on his hand.

Two years ago during winter, there was dense fog on the highway my father was driving on. The vehicles were going in a single line. Suddenly an animal came in front of one of the vehicles, and the driver applied emergency brakes. All the vehicles behind him bumped into the vehicle in front of them. My father's legs got jammed between the seat and the steering wheel due to which he was once again admitted to a hospital for a month. And again, the truck owner deducted ₹10,000 from his salary for the damage to the glass, radiator and the body of the truck. He also fired my father from his job. Because of this, the expenses of the hospital had to be borne by my father by taking a loan. He also had to bail himself out after the police registered a case against him. The truck owner got the truck bailed out but did not bail out my father.

In spite of all these hardships, my father is providing us with good education. In fact, he teaches us all to never lose heart. We have learnt from our father that we should work very hard. We have faced many difficulties, but it is said that everyone faces difficulties and he who copes with difficulties is a real man.

29

The Risky Road

Marri Mamatha

My story is about the incidents my father encountered on the road. My father is a truck driver. His suffering from liver damage shows how irregular work-shifts spoil the health of a long-haul truck-driver. In addition, truck drivers have to face all kinds of risks—from armed robbers to hazards on the road.

My father has been attacked several times during his long trips. One night he was transporting goods worth lakhs to deliver at a faraway location. Suddenly he spotted some people putting up a barricade on the road with a couple of logs. He had no option but to stop. Before he knew it, the men forced open the cabin door and started beating him. My father did not have much money on him, and this agitated the robbers so much that they beat him black and blue. He was badly injured.

Another time, bike-borne miscreants chased him. When he sensed trouble, he tried to speed away. But they took out guns and started firing at the lorry. My father had to surrender to save his own life. That day he thought of giving up his job. But quitting is not so easy for a driver who has to look after a family with three children. He continued driving to make sure that all of us got proper education. He does not want us to go through hardships like him.

The scariest incident happened the day a biker-gang chased his loaded lorry on a highway in the wee hours of the morning. He tried to drive faster but they overtook him. Two of them blocked the road, forcing him to step on the brake. They tried to open the door from outside but could not do that. Finally, they smashed the window to get into the cabin. They held both my father and the cleaner at knife-point, and demanded money. When my father refused, they started beating him. A scuffle broke out as he was not ready to give up easily. At some point, they almost tried to stab him with the knife. Fortunately, he was able to snatch the knife from them and throw it outside. In the end though, he had to submit to their demand.

After they left, having robbed him of all the money he had, he broke into tears. Those few thousand rupees meant a lot to him. He wanted to save that for us, his children.

Accidents are quite common for long-distance drivers. One day my father was transporting coal to some place. He had to cross a bridge over a river on the way, but the condition of the bridge was bad. He lost control, hit the railing of the bridge and fell into the river along with the loaded lorry. Fortunately, it was winter, and the water was not too deep. Villagers from the nearby villages rescued him. Later, the lorry was pulled out with the help of cranes.

Long-distance driving is typically a job full of troubles. My father has to face some or the other trouble every day. Problems could be a little less for him if the roads were safer and properly maintained. It is not just unpredictable weather conditions that make driving dangerous. Poorly maintained roads which are full of potholes create high-risk situations too.

My father has the experience of driving both during the day and night. Night driving is obviously unsafe. It is only to raise his children well that he takes on all these troubles. But, we the family members start feeling very worried if he does not return home on time, especially when he is not able to make a phone call to us.

A truck driver is never able to spend enough time with his family. Being busy with his duty far away from home, my father has not attended many family events. We miss him so much at such times!

We learned the significance of following the right path from my father. He tells us how important it is for drivers to always follow traffic rules and signals, especially the speed limits. He wishes that proper signages are installed on roads and that drivers are trained to read them.

The other thing he always emphasises on is our

education. Only studying well can get us good jobs and create better living conditions for ourselves, he tells us.

My father is proud of his three daughters. I thank Mahindra Truck and Bus for this initiative to support the daughters of truck drivers. A supportive environment will empower people like us, who belong to disadvantaged families, to serve our own families as well as the country in the future.

30

The Ulcer

Ayesha Begum

I always pray for the safety and well-being of my father. If our father does not come back home on time, we keep waiting for him, while disturbing thoughts run through our minds: What could have happened to Papa? Why has he not come yet? Is he okay or not? Is there something wrong with the vehicle? Where could Papa be? What would he be doing?

It is not for nothing that we worry so much about him.

An incident happened in the year 1995. At that time, my father used to drive a rice lorry for the rice mill of Guru Raghvendra in Mandya. On that day my father and his cleaner had gone to fetch rice from Devarkadra. While they were loading the truck it started raining. They were covering the truck with a tarpaulin and tying it with a rope when my father felt severe pain in his stomach. Despite the pain he continued to fix the tarpaulin. And in such a state, he drove the truck to a nursing home near Devarkadra.

The doctor gave him some medicines, but it was of

no use. Somehow, my father left the hospital and drove back to the rice mill. As he turned off the engine of his vehicle, the cleaner ran up to the owner and told him about my father's condition. By that time, my father was feeling much worse. He could not even straighten his legs. He was unable to sit in a car, and the owner had to practically call for help to lift him from the lorry and make him lie down inside a jeep.

They took him to a hospital in Narayanpet to get him treated by our family doctor. The doctor referred him to the district hospital where scans and reports showed his condition to be very serious. An ulcer had burst inside his stomach and the poison could spread in his body if not operated upon immediately, they said. On hearing this, my father's boss gave the doctors permission to operate on him. By the time we reached the hospital, my father had already been operated upon. He was discharged after a few days and was under treatment for three months. Soon after that, he was back on the road and driving.

It is hard to believe now how my father drove in such pain. But he did. Just so that his four daughters are well provided for, that we are all educated and able to cope with the difficulties of life successfully. I love him so much, my papa.

31

My Father, My Teacher

Tabassum Begum

My father has been driving a lorry for forty years. He is the sole working member in our family, and yet, he has been able to provide for us. Though he is only a lorry driver, he has educated me, my three sisters and brother. This, when in our village girls rarely get any education.

We always pray for his safety and well-being. And sometimes, when he is late in coming home, we all get very worried. At other times, he comes home in the middle of the night, sometimes at around two in the morning, but we are not able to meet him as we are all asleep. My mother, however, stays awake and keeps waiting for him. We have faith in my father's driving because he follows all the rules and regulations but there are situations where even he is helpless. Like when his vehicle is stranded in a forest or during the rains or when he has to cope with vehicles coming from the opposite side at night.

The other day my father had gone to Assam. He was sleeping in his lorry after parking it in a hilly area when he heard some noise. The stones kept before the vehicle tyres had moved and his vehicle had suddenly started sliding down the slope. My father immediately woke up the cleaner and asked him to get down. The latter complied. Then my father tried his best to stop his vehicle from rolling back but it was impossible because the slope was very steep. With no other alternative, he turned his vehicle towards a tree and the vehicle bumped into its trunk. My father was grievously injured, but he still drove the lorry on to the road and to his destination.

Once, when my father was taking a lorry full of stones to Hyderabad, he was stuck behind another lorry which was not letting him pass. It wasn't even allowing an ambulance to overtake it, even though its sirens were blaring. Then my father steered his lorry to a side lane with great difficulty and let the ambulance pass. Further down, he also let a car in which a family was travelling move ahead of him.

We have learnt from my father to never break the rules. The second thing he has taught us is the value of hard work. No matter what the weather is like—scorching heat, pouring rain or freezing cold—he works. A common man may get a sunstroke, catch a cold or fever, and may take an off, but not my father. He always worries about us but hardly thinks about his own health, even though he has been operated upon thrice. The doctors have forbidden him from driving but my father still drives his lorry because that is his only means of livelihood. I am very thankful to my father and love him very much.

32

Be Cautious, Avert Accidents

Khusbu Kumari

We are a family of four. Besides me, there is my younger brother, Monu, my mother and my father. I am pursuing my graduation while my brother, who is five years younger to me, studies in eleventh standard. My brother and I go to school/college together; both are far away from our house at Havaspur village in Beguserai district, which is about five kilometres from the district headquarters. My father, who is a driver by profession, drives an oil tanker for the Barauni Refinery. Whenever my father is at home, I am the happiest person, because he takes my brother and me for a stroll to the nearby market. The times when he is not at home are the hardest for us because we don't know when we will see him next.

Recently my father was informed that he had to take his vehicle to Bengal. My father got ready and took off in a jiffy, and for some reason, he could not call us that day. In the evening, my mother asked me to call him up but his phone was switched off. Just so she would not get tense, I told Mother that it appears as though the phone is not charged. But my mother looked worried. We did not sleep well that night as we were waiting for his call. However, our phone rang only the next morning. It was my father on the other side. All at once, we were very happy. My mother, who was in the kitchen, came and stood beside me. After talking to me, my father talked to my mother for a long time. Something was wrong, I knew, for she looked very sad after the call ended. When I asked her, she said it was nothing. In the evening, my brother and I finished studying and went to bed after dinner.

Early next morning, I awoke to the voice of my father. He was telling my mother why he didn't call and why his phone was switched off. It so happened that a strong wind was blowing when he started his journey, and soon after that, it started to rain. At about ten in the night, his tanker collided with another vehicle coming from the opposite direction. My father applied the brakes and stopped his tanker on the left side of the national highway. He jumped down from the tanker and ran to help the driver of the other vehicle, quite unmindful of his mobile phone which was in his pocket and got damaged because of the rain. The driver of the other vehicle was injured and crying in pain; both his legs were broken and he had severe head injuries. The latter soon became unconscious. After leaving his vehicle in the care of his co-driver, my father took a lift from another passenger vehicle and got this driver admitted to the Sadar hospital, and didn't leave until the doctors had told him that the man was out of danger.

By the time the other driver regained consciousness, it was next morning. The injured driver told my father how he was talking to his family on the mobile phone because of which he didn't pay enough attention to the road and collided with my father's truck. My father informed this driver's family about his well-being and returned to his tanker, safe and happy to be driving back home.

33

Lies Trail Behind

Bharti

It was the year 2001. One day my father was driving his truck towards Narnaul from Sonepat. There he filled the vehicle with a load of mustard and went out to Faizabad. After unloading all the goods there he drove back to the transport company and left for Calcutta after loading his truck with sugar. It was a four-day drive from Faizabad to Calcutta. There were no mobile phones those days. My father thought that he would call us later from an STD booth. But as he went along he found that all the STD phones on the way were out of order. There was obviously some problem with the phone lines.

On the day that my father had left Faizabad for Calcutta the transport company called us on the landline. They said, 'Your father's truck has fallen into the gulf in Sasaram (Bihar). Your father is in the hospital and he is not in any condition to speak.'

We were shocked. My mum was alone at home and

she was in great distress. At that time, we three sisters were very small. Upon hearing the news of my father's accident, our whole family was in mourning. Our relatives arranged for a vehicle and went to Sasaram to find my dad and his truck. And when they didn't find the truck, they went to the police station. But no complaint had been lodged there. The police didn't have a clue as to who my father was.

In panic and confusion, my mum called the transport company repeatedly, trying to gather information about my father and his truck. Three days later, my father arrived at the Calcutta transport company office. There the transporter told him that according to some information given to them his truck had met with an accident! My father asked him not to utter such inauspicious words. The office people advised my father to call home immediately. The call came at around 5 p.m. All our relatives were present in our house at that time. My aunt answered the phone call. On hearing my father's voice, she could not believe that it was actually my father speaking. She told him about all that had happened. My dad assured her that he was absolutely fine and that no accident had taken place. Somebody must have made a false call. Upon hearing this my family breathed a sigh of relief. Everyone asked him to come home as soon as possible.

But because of the fake call, my mother has had to take medicine till date to maintain her blood pressure.

If my dad had had a mobile phone at that time or if he had made a call from an STD booth, then maybe my family would not have suffered so much.

34

Caution Saves

T. Latha

My father has fifteen years of experience in driving a lorry on long routes. He has been working for a private transport company for many years. He is frequently praised by his employer for his sincerity and punctuality. Some of the other drivers drink liquor, risking their lives while driving. But my father never drinks. He ardently follows safe driving rules. Most of the drivers rush while returning from the delivery location. But my father does not mind taking an extra hour, and keeps speed under permissible limits which helps prevent accidents.

This is one story from the chronicles of my father's long driving experience.

My father once had to drive all night on a route different from the usual one. At around four in the morning, he felt sleepy. He parked the vehicle safely under a tree, approximately a hundred feet away from the edge of the road. Then he fell asleep inside his cabin.

After half an hour or so, he heard a loud sound somewhere nearby. He rushed out of his cabin to find that a public bus carrying many passengers had crashed into a truck, which was parked close to the edge of the road.

The lorry driver died on the spot. A few passengers in the bus had been injured too. The lorry driver had been driving all alone; there was no other helper. He had probably felt sleepy.

My father had a narrow escape that day. It could have been his truck too! He normally parks his vehicle at the side of the road. If he had done so on that day, he would have met the same fate. It was a big relief for us that nothing happened to him, but at the same time, we felt sorry for the affected ones. A simple incautious step by a long-distance lorry driver can lead to such a terrible accident. Parking on the road is a common mistake almost all lorry drivers make. They should always park their lorries in a space that is a little far from the main road, either in a parking bay or in a location where moving vehicles do not enter.

Driver fatigue accounts for a number of fatal accidents on the road. Irregular work schedules, insufficient sleep and long hours of work make drivers tired and drowsy. When they pressurise themselves to work in that condition, accidents are almost certain to happen. Sleep is necessary. Taking a break from work and taking a nap for as little as half an hour plays a big role in safe driving. Reaching the destination is important. Reaching late is, obviously, better than not reaching at all! No one is immune to danger on the road. But a little caution can always prevent fatalities.

35

An Ideal Father

Jeevarekha Aanbalagan

My grandfather, father, uncles and cousins are truck drivers. Driving is the most favoured occupation in my family. Trucks are like demigods to us. I am really happy and proud to say that I am the daughter of a driver. There are six members in my family—my father, mother, two younger sisters, younger brothers, and me. My father is forty-seven years old, and is still working hard so that we have a comfortable life.

In 1993, my father met with an accident near Haveri. This led to a major surgery on his nose. He still has a deep scar on his face. On another occasion when he was driving at night, some thieves appeared from nowhere, threatened him with dire consequences and took away ₹12,500 from his bag. They stabbed him in his leg with a knife and for six months he suffered from that injury. After this incident, he tries to avoid driving alone at night. In spite of these troubles, he never ever gave up his faith in the vehicle or lost his confidence in driving.

Road hazards keep him worried, but he doesn't tell us a thing. My mother suffers from the uncertainty of this profession too. Whenever he is travelling, she prays for his safety. But she, too, hides her concerns from her children, so that our focus doesn't shift from our studies.

In 2014, my grandfather expired. At that time, my father was in North India. He could not see his father during those last moments. It was heart-breaking to see him crying, once he was back. He still grieves about not being there when his father breathed his last. He misses his father so much.

My father tells me, 'Don't be afraid of anything, because it is your life, you have to live for yourself. Don't cheat anyone. If you cheat by a rupee, know that you will end up losing ten times more. So be true to yourself and your surroundings. As a girl child, you are the backbone of your family. So be brave and be honest, help others with what you have.'

For my father I am his hope. He thinks he couldn't do anything special for his nation because of the limitations of his profession. Circumstances didn't allow him to go to school. 'But, now I am always there for you. I want my daughter to become an IAS officer,' he says.

He often stops his vehicle near the collector's office and tells his co-drivers that his daughter is also studying to become an IAS officer!

His words are strongly inscribed in my heart. My ambition is to become an IAS officer. I am currently pursuing Electronics and Communication engineering, but after I complete my course, I will definitely write the UPSC examination. I am also interested in the Scouts and Guides activities. I recently received the Rajya Puraskar Award from Bharat Scouts and Guides.

To help and save people from accidents, my sister is studying Accident and Emergency Care technology. My mother, too, helps the drivers from other states, by preparing food for them during strikes. Once, my father spent two days without food in Kerala. That experience has made my parents sensitive about the basic needs of the people coming from other states.

My father is a super hero to my family. My mother is a beautiful companion to my father. I am trained today to be brave and happy while facing all the struggles of life.

36

Sigh of Relief

Sarvleen Kaur

My papa is an exceptional gift given to us and without him the definition of the word 'family' would be incomplete for us.

My story dates back to five years ago. It was the morning of 23 May 2013. My sister, Kikki, and I were getting ready for school. My mother was preparing food and packing our tiffin. Suddenly, Tavan, my cousin, rushed into the room. He was sweating excessively and his heart was beating like a woodpecker continuously knocking on a tree trunk.

When I saw him, I got frightened. To calm him down I offered him a glass of water and asked him softly, 'What happened, Tavan?' He replied in a low voice, 'Didi, Chachu got trapped near a river with his truck. While he was trying to handle the situation, the tyre of the truck exploded and he fell on the road, injuring himself severely. He has been admitted to the local hospital where the treatment is going on.'

When we heard this, we froze. We were in complete shock. The light of our life, the pillar of our family, was injured. Tears rolled down my cheeks.

Meanwhile, Taya ji, my uncle, entered the room and saw us crying. He consoled us by saying that Tavan knows only half the truth. Papa was actually fine now and had been discharged from the hospital. Taya ji informed us that Papa would be arriving at Jammu Airport by 2 p.m. and would be with us soon.

We eagerly awaited his return. Taya ji and I went to the airport to pick up Papa. The plane landed on time. We kept a constant eye on the gate. I was so excited that by then I knew the position of the smallest object over there.

After some time, the passengers started coming out from the gate. Between unknown faces, I saw one sporting a black turban; he was wearing a white check shirt, and I jumped with joy.

I believe that I was born twice. First, as a baby girl on 18 September and then again on the afternoon of 23 March when my papa returned to me, safe and sound. I hugged him tightly and started crying. I felt so relieved. It was as if all my shattered dreams had become whole again and resurfaced on seeing Papa.

Telling those you love how you feel before it's too late and living every day like it is your last day, now had a new meaning for me.

Experiences teach us great things in life. My father's

experiences always make me stronger. They teach me to never give up. I learned that life sometimes offers you tough challenges but the real warrior is the one who goes through them and never gives up. Honesty is the best way to lead a content life and is the most precious gift of God. I have learned from my father to help others and stand by others during hardships. His experiences have made me what I am today.

37

The Bus and the Truck

Guntas Kaur

In ancient times, there were no facilities for travelling. Later, man invented the wheel to increase the speed of human movement from one place to another. Rather than walking, they started using bullock carts, etc. The next invention was the steam engine. The combination of an engine and wheels resulted in vehicles. Motor vehicles play a major role in our lives. Today there are many means of transportation that we take by either road, air, water, or by rail. But mostly we travel by road in our day-to-day lives. And yet, like two sides of every coin, there are many hazards of road travel too. Carelessness on the road can result in accidents, which can cause injuries or death. Today because of the increase in road transportation, road safety has become a very important issue in India.

My dad is a truck driver. Years back, when he was driving from Mansar towards Jammu, his truck met with an accident. The truck was carrying sheep and goats.

The owner of the animals was also present with my dad. Suddenly, when my dad was driving over a bridge, he saw an out-of-control, overloaded bus struggling to stay on the road. Instantly, my father thought he must save the passengers in the bus. He managed to hit the bus in such a way that the bus stopped. But due to the weight of the bus and the impact, the truck skidded, turned turtle and stopped after taking two turns, on a heap of sand. Fortunately, my father and the owner of the sheep and goats were safe and sustained only minor injuries.

My father works day and night to earn his living, to educate me and give us a comfortable life. He gives me every single thing I want. But when he doesn't return home on time, the family gets very worried. Terrible thoughts come to our minds. I end up feeling that something might have happened to my dad. I feel worried and scared. In newspapers we read reports about distracted drivers, over-speeding, drunk driving, reckless driving, jumping traffic signals, under-age drivers, driving on the wrong side, or on one-way streets, driving under the influence of drugs and alcohol, animals crossing the roads, and more. So many accidents are caused by heavy rains, snowstorms, road rage, potholes, fog, and other conditions.

My father, though, remains untouched by such reports. Or at least that's how he behaves in front of us. He has been driving a truck for twenty years now. He has learnt from experience how to avoid danger. 'Always keep your mind calm. You should know what to do in an emergency situation. Be alert while driving and keep your eyes focussed on the road. Only if you can think quickly and effectively can you overcome the threats that life on the road can throw at you,' he says. Our lives' journey rests on his confidence in his brakes and steering wheel, and our confidence in his driving.

38

Worries Trail Behind

Konathala Doctor Vijaya Noora Aparna

Think of a situation when a family member hasn't returned home, and you can't communicate with him. You have no clue where he is, with whom, or whether he is safe. God forbid!

For my family though, this is a usual scenario. It frequently happens that my father is late or is away for days and we have no information about him. Either the networks are jammed or he is unable to take calls because he is busy with his work. All we can do is pray for his safety and hope that things are fine with him. When we try to call him and he doesn't respond, we are unable to sleep that night. A thousand questions keep rising in our minds. What could have happened? Why did he not answer our calls? Why did he not tell us he would be late? What to do now? Of course we have faith in his driving but still we worry about him.

My father usually drives at a speed of 40 kmph. Only during emergency situations does he increase his speed.

He never forgets his driving licence, load details or papers related to the goods he is carrying, insurance papers, pollution check certificate, etc. He always prays before setting out on a journey. He prefers not to drive during late hours and tries to come back by 12.30 in the night.

Years of driving has taught him a lot about trucks. These days if there is any problem with the vehicle while driving, he resolves it himself, because he knows how to repair a truck pretty well. 'Why waste time waiting for the mechanic? At times their delay in reaching me affects my performance. After all, he will not bear the brunt if I am not able to deliver the load on time. The mechanics are casual and relaxed, but I get tense with each passing moment. Better to depend on oneself than on anyone else. My life, my work, my responsibility!' he says. These days if anyone else needs his help on the way, be it another truck driver or a passenger car, he instantly helps them out in whatever way he can.

However, while on the road one doesn't know what might happen. Things are unpredictable. Sometimes, even if we do not make any mistakes, accidents occur. At times he is not allowed entry in some cities. He has to wait for long periods of time to get clearance in such situations. In other cases it is the weather that causes delays. Recently, he was stranded in West Bengal due to floods.

My father takes every kind of safety precaution while driving. His juniors often come to him, seeking advice.

He has trained some of the elders too. He keeps them informed about safety precautions, responsible driving, how to drive on narrow roads, etc. 'Never overload your vehicle,' he tells them. 'Overloading is very dangerous. A large number of accidents have occurred due to this, but we don't realise it.' At times he turns to me for suggestions. The internet is handy with information on self-help techniques while driving late at night, or to find out about the weather conditions on the route he has to follow, and at his destination, or government rules regarding entry into cities and permits, etc. I try to help him out by looking for the information and sharing it with him. He is just as happy to learn from me, as I have learnt from him all my life.

My father's experiences on the roads have been a part of my growing-up process. Books have not taught me what the stories from my father's life have.

39

An Unfair Journey

Farhen Sultana

If you think your life is tough, then please allow me to describe some incidents which will tell you about a truck driver's life. After all, who would know it better than me, a truck driver's daughter!

I particularly remember the day when my father met with an accident. He was driving through a remote village when a goat suddenly jumped in front of his truck and got crushed under its wheels. Within minutes, the village people surrounded him and started shouting at him. They pulled him down from the vehicle and began to beat him up as if it was his mistake. The unruly crowd refused to hear a word from him. Luckily, a person who knew my father came to his rescue and pacified the mob. My father called the owner of the truck, who paid the compensation for the goat to its owner, and took my father for medical treatment. The mob had beaten him so badly that his hand was fractured and he was on bed rest for two months after that.

There have been many such occasions when my father has been ill-treated or held hostage for no fault of his. Once, he was driving his truck very fast, because the goods had to reach their destination in time. Some people simply assumed that he was driving like that because he was drunk and had hit someone. They shouted and gathered a big crowd which stopped the truck and tried to assault my father. My father apologised for driving fast, asked them to forgive him and let him go so that he could resume his journey. He told them that he had never consumed alcohol in his life, but they wouldn't believe him.

It was a terribly humiliating experience for an honest, poor, law-abiding man. The incident affected not just him, but the entire family! Whenever my father doesn't return home on time, all these old memories resurface. We are under immense stress. Has he met with an accident? Has he faced some problem? We keep wondering. The worst fears keep hovering in our minds, and we pray to God for his safe return.

As we stay in the town area, heavy vehicles like trucks, buses, etc., are only allowed before 7 a.m. or after 7 p.m. If someone tries to drive heavy vehicles during day time, they are detained and fined by the traffic police. However, driving after sunset is not all that easy. Often, robbers block the roads with logs or stones. When the truck drivers stop to clear the road, the robbers loot their goods, money, watches or anything else they can get their hands on. Worse, the driver and his assistant are sometimes murdered and the vehicle stolen. This has happened with other truck drivers we have known, and it sends a chill down my spine every time my father steps out on duty.

Due to natural calamities my father faces many difficult situations. Sometimes he has to drive in hilly areas during the rainy season. There, landslides are common and increase the risk of accidents. And then there was a time when my father had to drive at night through areas that were flooded. The wheels refused to move smoothly through water-logged areas. In such conditions when the vehicle breaks down or needs servicing, it is very difficult to find a mechanic. With most of the dhabas and hotels closed because of the weather, my father had to drive without food.

Another hazard is the one that arises during festivals and pujas, when some devotees stop vehicles and demand donations from drivers. If the drivers refuse, these devotees try to harass them in other ways, which makes it difficult to drive ahead.

My father is a truck driver and works very hard to give us the best education, so that we become responsible citizens. Many people might have some wrong impressions about truck drivers, and they nurture strange prejudices formed out of baseless presumptions. It is grossly unfair and sometimes cruel because the truck drivers are simple, hardworking people who risk their lives for their families.

I can't change society all by myself. But I will definitely contribute my bit to changing people's attitudes towards truck drivers. I will educate people to form their ideas logically instead of bringing suffering on someone by blaming them unfairly or criticising them. But first I will study well, and take up a job to relieve my father from his endless trials.

40

The Drive of Life

G. Archana

My father has been driving for almost thirty years now. When he was twelve years old, he started working as a cleaner of trucks and continued to do that for eight years. He became a driver in the year 1987. He has driven all across India—from Kolkata, Delhi, and Nagpur to Mysore, Hyderabad and many other places.

Whenever my father goes out on duty he returns home only after twenty to twenty-five days. We have missed him on several festivals and family functions. He often goes without proper food and basic necessities, which worries us a lot. But despite all that, he works very hard to drive and transport goods safely and quickly.

My father had explained to me that his job is not just driving a vehicle, but to successfully deliver goods within a specified period of time. His role is important in that ecosystem, as the goods can be processed only after he delivers them. 'Yes, I have to drive day and night, but that's the nature of my work. If I miss the delivery deadline then chances are that the goods will get spoiled and I will be fined for that. But more importantly, with my delay or negligence, many other people's hard work might go down the drain, and an entire system would suffer!' he told me.

At times I wonder, does the system care for him equally? He works really hard, but seldom does he get the credit and respect he deserves.

God forbid, my father has never faced any road accident because he remains very careful while driving. But he has witnessed many road accidents.

When he had travelled to Hyderabad some time ago, a newly married couple along with their relatives were driving back after the marriage ceremony. The van met with an accident and all the people were severely injured. One person's head was smashed, some had fractured limbs, and some lost their fingers. The newly married couple was also seriously injured. My father and his friends stopped their vehicles to rescue the passengers in the van, gave them whatever first aid they could and called the ambulance. That accident had occurred because the driver was drunk. My father still says that it was the most horrifying accident he has ever seen in his driving experience. I can see the pain on his face when he talks about it even now. Memories of that tragedy affect him even though so much time has passed by.

I look at his sadness and wonder how safe he was when immediately after attending to the victims of that terrible accident he had to take the steering wheel and drive off to his destination! Perhaps it takes nerves of steel, or something more that can't be put in words.

In the last thirty years of his driving career, he has seen mishaps occurring because of drunk driving. There have been times when he has forced his friends to stop the vehicle and take a few hours of rest when they seemed to be sleepy while driving. This is a precaution he takes to avoid accidents and drive safely on the roads. Yet, sadly, a truck driver hardly gets the sleep he needs because most of the time, he drives all day. Stopping at night is also risky, he says, because robbers pose a serious threat. 'Things can turn fatal if we are not careful,' he adds.

As I said before, my father drives for long distances. At times, he says that it'll take him a few days to come back home, but when he doesn't, my family and I become very worried about him. Fifteen years ago, there were no means of communication. My father could only call and inform the nearest person with a telephone to pass on a message to us. There were no mobiles in those days.

I am still learning from my father, the art of driving, not just a truck but also life. He tells me, 'In any condition, we should work hard and always be ready to solve the problem in hand. Put your best foot forward to fill your life with happiness.'

41
I Shall Fly

Gokila Priya

We are a loving family of four from Namakkal in Tamil Nadu—my father, mother, sister and I. Being the older of the two children, I am expected to take care of my family in the absence of my father. 'Absence of my father' could mean for a day or a longer period at a stretch. Truck drivers don't have a predictable schedule. My sister and I miss him every day and even more when we see our friends' fathers coming to pick them up from school. Generally, parents pray for their children but in our house we pray for our father and for his safety, as we eagerly wait for him to come back home.

And that is not all. I have cried so many times after hearing his experiences while driving on the road.

Two years ago, while driving through the remote areas of North India where the roads are uneven and badly maintained, my father's vehicle met with an accident. Not only was he seriously injured, his vehicle was also damaged. We were waiting for father to reach home and were worried when he didn't. There wasn't any way to contact him because he was driving through the interiors where mobile networks don't exist. After two days he came back wrapped in bandages. He had injuries all over his body. We were shocked to see him in that condition. But by God's grace he was safe.

That scene of my father limping in pain has left a deep scar on my mind.

My father has a difficult time when the weather is bad, especially if it is raining. I hate monsoons just because of this. There are times when the wipers of the lorry don't work properly because of the heavy rain but my father continues to drive through all the thunder and lightning. He doesn't have the luxury to park and wait for the sky to clear. Such is the nature of his work.

My father has told me many stories about his trips, which have astonished and shocked me. Once, he was driving on a highway with a co-driver. As they got down to freshen up, a group of robbers came and stole money from the lorry leaving my father helpless. Sadly, instead of empathising with him, the owner of the vehicle scolded him for being so 'careless'.

As a driver's daughter, I know that 'moving on' is the philosophy of our lives. I have grown up with my father, absorbing a lot of his feelings and understanding his approach towards life. I am not surprised that he wants his children to be achievers in life. He's always encouraging me and my sister to study well and become independent.

I am a student of MSc (Physics). My ambition is to become a scientist and fulfil my father's wishes. In the future I want to make my father's journey easier and satisfying. I just hope that day is not too far away!

42

The Jail Term

K.M. Habiba Naaz

It was the second Sunday of January 2008. I was enjoying the holiday with my friends at home. They used to come over every Sunday and we would play indoor games. That day we were having a lot of fun playing hide and seek. My friend Anam was hiding in the kitchen where my mum was busy making aloo parathas for us. That was when my mother's phone started to ring.

She picked up the call and after a few moments of patient hearing, said, 'Oh God, how did this happen?' It was my father on the other side of the call. All of us immediately gathered near the kitchen, waiting for my parents' conversation to be over. When she disconnected the phone, my mum said grimly, 'Your father got arrested by the Assam police.'

Shocked, I asked, 'Why, what has he done?'

Mum shook her head. 'Nothing. It was not his mistake.'

I requested my mother to explain things more clearly to me. My friends were also waiting anxiously.

'Your father was driving the truck and some mischievous boys, who were drunk, came in front of the truck. Your father tried to swerve the truck in another direction but he could not as the river was flowing on both sides of the road. The boys have got seriously injured; one of them died on the spot. The police has arrested your father and put him in prison.' My mother's voice sank, as she spoke. 'No one came to render any help to your father. Now the police is slapping and beating him. He is not able to tell them that it was not his fault, as the police in that area does not understand the language he speaks!'

On the second day, my father was produced before the court. But unfortunately, the official language of the court was English, and my father does not understand English. He could not defend himself. So the court easily passed a judgement against my father that sentenced him to two years in jail. That was when I realised how big a role education and language play in our life. If my father knew English, this situation would not have arisen.

That day, I just kept thinking again and again about my father and how he is innocent and how he will be facing the worst period of his life. That day was a black day for us. We forgot all about our lunch when we heard this terrible news. But the worst day gave me the best source of motivation in the strangest possible way. I stood up to face the problem by taking it positively.

On that day, I committed to learn the English language.

I started working hard to learn English so that such a situation would never arise again.

How we spent those two years I can't explain in words. At the end of the most ruthless testing period, when my father was about to return home, all our relatives and neighbours came to visit us with sweets and lots of prayers. My brother, mother and I went to Assam Central Jail to bring him back home. I received my father at Gate Number 1 of Assam Central Jail with the English words, 'Welcome home Papa.'

43

The Overturn

Deepa

My father has experienced a number of road accidents. In 1993, while he was travelling from Belgaum to Erode in a Comet lorry on the highway near Haveri, the roads had become slippery due to heavy rains. It was there that my father's lorry overturned. He incurred severe head and nose injuries. Many a time, my father has been chased by thugs in two-wheelers while driving at night. Once, he sustained injuries and cuts on his right leg when thieves riding motorbikes looted ₹12,500 from him.

There are several risks that truck drivers have to take while driving in the night for days on end. Driving through the night often leads to eye pain and body aches, besides the constant fear of being chased or attacked by robbers. I wish there was a rule that does not permit one to drive after 11 p.m.; it will benefit the drivers and avert many road accidents or robberies that happen during night-time. I also believe that a truck driver should always be accompanied by another person during the journey. That's not only for safety but also for help during emergencies.

My father had witnessed the difficulties my grandfather, who was also a truck driver, underwent. To help my grandpa, my father left school after Class IX and got the job of a lorry cleaner. But a driver's license is accorded to only those who have passed the secondary examinations. Anyway, after a few years of hard work, he became a driver and eventually the owner of his truck. But he has to be away from the family for a long time. When my grandpa expired my father was unable to come in time to see his own father one last time. I can still see that sorrow, guilt and remorse, for not being able to come for my grandpa's last rites, writ large on his face.

Now that I am older I understand that some rules must be enforced, and some changed. If, for example, irrespective of the person's educational qualifications, the driver's license is issued after ensuring that the candidate is properly trained in driving, then more people can get jobs as truck drivers.

In our own family, the truck my father worked so hard to own, is helping us in so many ways. By driving the truck he has resolved all our financial troubles. He had to sacrifice his studies to become a truck driver. But he insists that the four of us must be educated, whatever be the difficulties. He has put my elder sister through BE (ECE) and me into BSc (AECT). My younger sister is in Class XI, and younger brother in Class VIII.

According to my parents' wishes I will study well and help alleviate all the problems that my family has to go through. If I am asked who the best person in this world is, my answer will always be: 'My father.'

I have learnt from my father to have no fear, to take things lightly, not to get worked up or angry about anything, to work hard and be straightforward and honest with others. Also, I learnt how to help anyone in distress. And that's why I decided to study Accident and Emergency technology, so that I can help the victims of road accidents. I aspire to work in the accident and emergency care department and I will not deem it as work. Rather, I will consider it to be my responsibility, having seen my father and his colleagues suffer through poor emergency medical facilities year after year.

About the Authors

Nineteen-year-old **A. Deepa**, born to K. Anbalagan and A. Pavunambal, is pursuing her BSc in Accident and Emergency Care Technology at Nandha College of Allied Health Sciences. After completing college, she wants to stand by her family and dedicate herself to the welfare of accident victims by virtue of her profession.

Born to Shrafat and Malka, twenty-year-old **Aksha Khan** hails from Mathura, Uttar Pradesh. She is studying in Maharaja Agrasen Girls Inter College.

Young **Anujna Suvarna** lives with her parents, Divakar S. and Gayathri M., in Mangalore, Karnataka. A student of Sahyadri College of Engineering, seventeen-year-old

Anujna wants to be an innovator after she completes her education.

Born in Hasnabad, Telangana, twenty-four-year-old **Ayesha Begum** is the daughter of Md. Janangeer Ali and Saleema Begum. She is in her final year of graduation at Surya Laxmi Degree College, Narayanpet, and wants to pursue a career in teaching after the completion of her course.

Bersha Kumari from Begusarai in Bihar is a final year engineering student at Jayati Vidyapeeth Women's University, Jaipur. Presently, she is doing an internship with Tech Mahindra, Pune. She plans to do a Master's degree in engineering and then get her dream job at Mahindra as an engineer. Bersha believes in hard work and in holding one's head high under all circumstances. She understands her father really well and wishes to turn all his dreams for her into reality.

Twenty-year-old **Bharti** hails from Sonepat, Haryana. Born to Randheer Singh and Nirmala Devi, she aspires to be a successful English lecturer and translator. Currently she studies in GVM Girls' College, Sonepat.

Bhavna Gautam is the nineteen-year-old daughter of Virendra Kumar Gautam and Chamanlata. She is a second-year BA student at SDS Degree College in Kosi

Khurd, and plans to pursue a career in teaching after the completion of her course.

Bulbul Khan is an eighteen-year-old from Khamini village in Mathura, UP. Daughter of Guddi and Ravi Khan, Bulbul studies at RBS Degree College in Mathura and hopes to become a school teacher.

Born in Sundargarh, Odisha, twenty-two-year-old **Chitralaxmi Swain** is the daughter of Surendra and Manjulata Swain.

Twenty-year-old **D. Tejaswini** is from Kodad, Telangana. She is currently a second year BE student and aspires to help her family become more financially secure. Tejaswini is the daughter of D. Srinivas Rao and D. Anuradha.

Twenty-one-year-old **Farhen Sultana** was born to Mamtaz Begum and Khybar Ali. She is a resident of Kala Fakirtola Village in Nalbari district of Assam. She is pursuing her BA at Mahendra Narayan Choudhary Balika Mahavidyalaya, Nalbari.

Eighteen-year-old **G. Archana**, daughter of Gunasekaran and Annapoorani, hails from Modachor village of Erode district in Tamil Nadu. She is in her first year of college, and is studying Mathematics. She aspires to work in the banking sector in the future.

Gokila Priya from Namakkal, Tamil Nadu, is a student of Physics at Mahendra Arts and Science College. She is ambitious and driven and aspires to work at ISRO. Priya is proud of her father, a truck driver, and is determined to fulfil all his desires one day.

Twenty-year-old **Guntas Kaur** hails from Gandhinagar, Jammu. Born to Amarjeet Singh and Kuljeet Kaur, she aspires to be a chartered accountant. Currently, she is completing her Bachelor's degree in Commerce from Government College for Women in Jammu.

Gurdeep Kaur from Kathna city in Jammu and Kashmir, is in Class 12. She aspires to become an IAS officer and serve her country. Daughter of S. Popinder Singh and Mohinder Kour, she is sensitive to and aware of her role in making her life and that of her family and the people around her, better.

Eighteen-year-old **J. Maria Asuritha Riya** was born in Trichy, Tamil Nadu, and is the daughter of G. Jesudass and J. Lucia. She is pursuing her BCom degree at Holy Cross College and aspires to study chartered accountancy after the completion of her course.

Born to K. Aanbalagan and A. Pavunambal, twenty-one-year-old **Jeevarekha Aanbalagan** belongs to Sankari village of Salem district, Tamil Nadu. She is pursuing

BE (Electronics and Communication) at Knowledge Institute of Technology. Her aim is to join the Civil Services in the future.

Born in Bhognipur, UP, eighteen-year-old **Jiya**, is the daughter of Shakeel Ahmed and Rahmat Begum. She is in the final year of her degree course at Yashoda Kunwar Yadav Mahila Mahavidyalaya and plans to pursue an LLB after her graduation.

K.M. Habiba Naaz lives in Sambhal, Uttar Pradesh. Born to Md. Usman and Majda Nasreen, this seventeen-year-old aspires to become a teacher and help poor children have access to education. Currently she studies at the Ishrat Group of Institutes.

Born in Begusarai, Bihar, eighteen-year-old **Khusbu Kumari**, is the daughter of Hare Ram Pandit and Sheela Pandit. She is pursuing her graduation from RSS College in Beguserai.

Seventeen-year-old **Konathala Doctor Vijaya Noora Aparna** lives in Anakapalli, Andhra Pradesh. Born to KVK Kameswara Rao and K. Kamala, she a spires to become an IAS officer. Currently, she is studying in Shri Krishna College, Narsipatnam.

Seventeen-year-old **Maganti Lavanya**, daughter of M. Venkaiah and Pavani, lives in Ramachandrapuram, Telangana, and studies at Gowthami Junior College. She wishes to study engineering and work as an engineer.

Born in Nandurbar, Maharashtra, twenty-four-year-old **Mali Puja Shivaji** is the daughter of Shivaji Bhika Mali and Sakhubai Shivaji Mali. She is a student of MSc (Biochemistry) at MJ College, Jalgaon. She is looking at pursuing a career in teaching or taking up a job in the government sector after her post graduation.

Twenty-year-old **Marri Mamatha** is the daughter of Marri Achaiah and Marri Alivelu. The family hails from Haliya village in Nalgonda district of Telangana. Marri is studying a paramedical course at Zeevana Para-Medical College. As a future paramedic, she dreams of supporting her parents as well as the less fortunate in society.

Born in Sonepat, Haryana, twenty-three-year-old **Meenakshi Saini** is the daughter of Uday Singh and Savitri Devi. She has just completed her BCom from GVM Girls College and plans to take up a suitable job in the government sector.

Daughter of Venkatappa and Kamalamma Poojari, **Mounika Poojari** is nineteen years old and hails from Tandur village in Vikarabad district of Telangana. She wants to become a teacher who inspires the next generation to serve the country.

Born in Sonipat, Haryana; twenty-three-year-old **Pooja Dahiya** is the daughter of Baljeet Singh and Sunita. She is a final year MCom student at Girls College, Kharkhauda, and wants to support her family as soon as she is able to do so.

Prableen Kaur is a resident of Gadigarh village in Jammu & Kashmir. She is the daughter of Amarpal Singh and Kuljeet Kour. Eighteen-year-old Prableen is pursuing a diploma in Civil Engineering. She not only aspires to become an efficient engineer but also wishes to qualify for the Civil Services.

Twenty-three-year-old **Priti Chaudhary** hails from Mathura, Uttar Pradesh. Her father Netra Pal Singh is a truck driver and her mother Mrs Sarvesh Devi is a housewife. Currently, Priti is studying for a Basic Training Certificate after which she will be able to teach school children. She aspires to be a teacher so that she can change the future of the coming generations.

Ramija Abdulgafar Shirgruppe is the daughter of Abdul Gaffar Adam Shirgruppe and Hasinabi. Born in Kolhapur, the twenty-two-year-old is pursuing a diploma in Computer Science from SOMB IT Management College.

Eighteen-year-old **Riya Dahiya** is the daughter of Bhagat Singh and Sumite Devi of Sonepat, Haryana. Riya is pursuing a BSc and wants to become a lecturer after completing her graduation. She also aims for a job as a police inspector.

Rukhasar Khan is doing her BSc at Shree Siddhi Vinayak Mahavidyalaya, Mathura. She and her sister, Bulbul Khan, want to study hard and do well to give their father a better life. Seventeen-year-old Rukhasar aims to work as a nurse after her graduation.

Sarvleen Kaur from Jammu is pursuing BSc from Government College for Women in Gandhinagar. Aiming to become an IAS officer, it is her dream to serve the nation and most importantly, foster morality and humanity in society. Daughter of S. Gurcharan Singh and Amit Kour, she wants to earn love and respect for herself and leave her footprints in the sands of time.

Born in village Chaitma, Chhattisgarh, twenty-one-year-old **Shahanaj Parveen**, is the daughter of Sheikh Hasamtulla and Hasina Begum. She is a second year BCom student at Bilaspur College. She wants to be a chartered accountant and join a bank after the completion of her course.

Sharmeen Parveen hails from Sambhal, UP. Currently, she is pursuing her graduation. She wants to become a teacher. Twenty-four-year-old Sharmeen is the daughter of M. Aarif and Najneen.

Born in Bhoseri, Maharashtra, twenty-one-year-old **Sonali Dyaneshwar Jamadar**, is the daughter of Dyaneshwar Arjun Jamadar and Saraswati Dyaneshwar Jamadar. A student of Commerce at Pune University, Sonali plans to appear for the MPSC exam and take up a government job.

Suneeta Singh is the daughter of Netrapal and Sarvesh Devi. The family hails from Mathura, Uttar Pradesh. Twenty-two-year-old Suneeta is pursuing her MA at Dr B.R. Ambedkar University, and also training for the Staff Selection Commission (SSC) at KO Campus Pvt. Ltd. She hopes to join the Indian Army in the future.

T. Latha is studying Food and Nutrition for her BSc degree in RVS College of Arts and Science. This twenty-year-old daughter of a truck driver hails from Coimbatore district, Tamil Nadu. She aspires to be a nutrition expert after her graduation.

T. Sivasri, daughter of S. Thangathilagan and T. Shanthi, is twenty-four years old. Her father drives a truck to support the family. Sivasri is currently pursuing an MBA from Madras University and plans to take up a government job or start her own business once she completes her degree, so that she can achieve something worthwhile in her life.

Tabassum Begum is the daughter of Jameel Pasha and Shabana Begum. She is from Tandur village of Rangareddy district in Telangana. Twenty-year-old Tabassum is in the second year of the degree course in People's Degree College. She wants to work as a teacher in a government educational institution in the future.

Twenty-two-year-old **Talwar Kshitjia Sukhdev** was born to Talwar Sukhdev Santappa and Talwar Bharati Sukhdev. The spirited girl from Kolhapur has just completed her graduation from Saraswati Foundation and is now busy preparing for competitive exams.

Twenty-year-old **Vatika Kumar** is from village Palra in Sonepat district of Haryana. She is the daughter of Ashok Kumar and Sumani Devi. She is currently pursuing her BSc at Gita Vidya Mandir Girls College, Sonepat, and wants to become a zoology lecturer.

Born in a village in Maharashtra, twenty-year-old **Waghamare Puja Dagadu** is the daughter of Waghamare Dagadu Mariba and Gandhabai. She is a BA student at Veer Wajekar ASC College, Phunde, and wants to pursue an MA degree after completing her graduation.

Twenty-one-year-old **Yasmeen**, daughter of Liaqat Ali and Kureisha Begum, is studying the Basic Training Certificate course from District Education and Training

Institute at Unnav, Uttar Pradesh. Yasmeen aspires to be self-sufficient and pursue further studies to ensure a bright future for herself and her family.